HEALING YOUR INNER CHILD

A STEP-BY-STEP GUIDE TO REPARENTING YOURSELF FOR PERSONAL GROWTH, EMPOWERMENT, AND RECLAIMING EMOTIONAL STABILITY

BOBBIE MALOY

This is a work of nonfiction. However, some of the names and personal characteristics of the individuals involved have been changed in order to disguise their identities. Any resulting resemblance to persons living or dead is entirely coincidental and unintentional.

The content contained within this book may not be reproduced, duplicated or transmitted without direct written permission from the author or the publisher.

Under no circumstances will any blame or legal responsibility be held against the publisher, or author, for any damages, reparation, or monetary loss, direct or indirect, due to the information contained within this book, either directly or indirectly. All effort has been executed to present accurate, up to date, reliable, complete information. Readers acknowledge that the author is not engaged in the rendering of legal, financial, medical or professional advice. As of the time of initial publication, the URLs displayed in this book link or refer to existing websites on the Internet. Vital Skills Press LLC is not responsible for, and should not be deemed to endorse or recommend, any website other than its own or any content available on the Internet (including but not limited to any website, blog page, or information pages) that is not created by Vital Skills Press.

Copyright © 2024 Bobbie Maloy
All rights reserved
Published in the United States by Vital Skills Press

Disclaimer Notice:
This book is not designed as medical advice. Please consult a licensed professional before attempting any techniques outlined in this book. If you are experiencing a medical or mental health emergency, please dial 911 or reach out to a qualified mental health professional.

ASIN B0CVQSK6P2 (eBook)
ISBN 979-8-9899614-0-5 (Paperback)
ISBN 979-8-9899614-1-2 (HC)

Library of Congress Cataloging-in-Publication Data
Library of Congress Cataloging-in-Publication application has been submitted.
Printed in the United States of America

TABLE OF CONTENTS

Introduction	5
1. HAVEN OF HEALING	11
Preparing Your Physical Sanctuary	13
Building Your Mental Space	14
How to Create an Anchor Point	16
Finding Your Peace	18
2. MEETING YOUR INNER CHILD	19
What *Is* the Inner Child?	21
The Seven Inner Child Archetypes	23
How to Spot Your Shadow	26
Neglect and Your Inner Child	29
Introduce Yourself to Yourself	29
Embrace Your Inner Child	31
3. FREE YOUR PLAYFUL SOUL	35
Is Your Inner Child Running Your Adulthood?	35
The Healing Journey	41
Healing Through Self-Acceptance	45
Exercise: Perceptual Positions	50
Exercise: Self-Acceptance Journal Prompts	53
4. THE POWER OF BOUNDARIES	55
Boundaries 101	55
Fuzzy or Non-Existent Boundaries	63
The Cost of Not Setting Boundaries	65
Does Your Inner Child Affect Your Boundaries?	67
How to Set Healthy Boundaries	70
Exercise: The First Time	78
The Bottom Line	80

5. REPARENT YOURSELF — 83
- What Your Inner Child Needs from You — 88
- The Journey of Reparenting — 90
- Living Up to the Expectations of Others — 91
- Exercise: A Letter to Your Inner Child — 93
- Exercise: A Letter from Your Inner Child — 94
- Exercise: Playdate with Your Inner Child — 95
- Exercise: Resolving Internal Conflict — 96

6. MASTER YOUR EMOTIONS — 99
- Emotions of Childhood — 100
- The Science of Emotions — 101
- The Power of Naming Emotions — 104
- Emotional Control—Why is it Necessary? — 106
- Emotional Intelligence — 107
- Exercise: Emotional Awareness Journaling Prompts — 113
- Exercise: Positive Outcomes and Future Pacing — 114
- Exercise: Naming Your Emotions — 116

7. WHO ARE YOU BECOMING? — 119
- Who Do You Want to Be? — 119
- Alignment of Neurological Levels — 125
- Embracing Imperfection — 133
- How to Embrace Imperfections — 135
- Signs You Are Healing Your Inner Child — 136
- Exercise: Circle of Excellence (Ring of Power)! — 137

Conclusion — 141
Acknowledgments — 145
Notes: — 147

INTRODUCTION

Jane walked into the office, ready to fight. The email from her boss simply said, "we need to talk about your project." This was all she needed after the day she'd had.

On her way to work, some jerk nearly took off her front bumper when he cut in front of her in traffic. Jane yelled a few choice phrases at him as she slammed her brakes and spilled her tea. *Great, now I have a giant stain on my blouse.* To top off her commute, someone took her favorite parking spot, and all the close spaces were taken. *Guess it will be a little hike from the back of the lot today.*

Inside, the building wasn't any better. They were upgrading a room down the hall from her office, so her morning was filled with sawing and banging, which didn't help her growing headache. If this day didn't get any better, she was going to scream.

Then, the email from her boss arrived in her inbox. It was just enough to send her over the edge. Jane was normally calm and composed, but something was just off today. She felt like she was walking a razor-thin line between exhaustion and snapping at whoever dared to cross her path. But if she really thought about it, it wasn't just today. This feeling has been growing for a while. Something had to give. She couldn't keep on like this. She couldn't continue to be ready to snap at a moment's notice.

Maybe you're in a similar situation. Perhaps you have witnessed your life go haywire as you battle outbursts, not understanding where they came from or a feeling like something is not quite right. Many of us deal with stressors like this our entire lives, but we don't take the time to figure out what's really bothering us. We decide it's better to put on our big girl panties and walk out into the world like nothing is wrong. But that only works for so long.

"Jane" was me several years ago. I had done my best to put on a brave face and power through my days, but I knew something was missing. I tried everything to fix the issue. I changed jobs, started working out, changed my sleep schedule, cut out a few extra activities, and nothing seemed to work. I was still walking the fine line between keeping it all together and unleashing a monster on the world.

It was exhausting. It wasn't until I was introduced to the concept of an inner child that I saw radical changes in how I approached the world and, more importantly, how my day-to-day interactions with everyone around me changed.

The fact is, we all have an inner child. And unfortunately, we also all have wounds from our childhood. For some, those wounds result from childhood trauma and abuse on levels many can't even comprehend. For others, there may not be any major traumatic events in our childhood, but there were little wounds created through normal, everyday interactions with our parents, siblings, friends, and other important people in our lives. You most likely had needs that weren't completely met or unheard emotions. These interactions can leave scars, even if they don't become clear until years later.

While we can't change the past, we can help our inner child through the situations they faced and, in return, guide them—and us—to much more successful outcomes in our adult lives. Recognizing the problem is the first step, but it is only a fraction of the issue.

This book is a compassionate guide that helps you navigate how to reparent your inner child. It holds the key to transformation and renewed inner peace. When you address past hurts and reconnect with your inner child, you will have the tools you need to live a more fulfilled and healed life.

The process I share is simple, and I have done my best to keep it that way. But there may be times it feels uncomfortable. Sometimes, it takes going back to your past to unlock a better future. You may stir up some old pain as you dig into your memories, but don't be afraid. It's okay to go through the process and exercises on non-traumatic memories in this book. The exercises will work even if you use them for a simple argument with a friend, the time you make a snide remark to your coworker, or even a word that triggers an unwanted response from you.

No matter what you work on or what you experience during the exercises, you are on the right track. The exercises put your subconscious mind—where your inner child lives—to work, so you may not always feel you are changing, but your subconscious is healing.

Anytime you do inner child work, it will require some self-compassion. You may tackle some hard feelings, so it's important that you remember to treat yourself with grace. There is no defined path everyone walks. Yours may look different from someone else's, and you may detour along the way. You may find that certain steps take you longer or that progress seems a little slow at first. This is perfectly natural and to be expected.

I have been where you are. I know what it's like to feel out of control, like something other than you is pulling your strings. It's what led me to this research. You are looking for answers and relief; that is what this book is all about.

There are so many instances where you'll use the techniques in this book. Are you having a difficult time with an overbearing coworker? There is a technique for that. Do you want to strengthen your relationships? We'll work on the steps you should take. You will be amazed at how many of your everyday struggles can be traced back to unaddressed wounds.

In the following pages, you'll work through exercises from a wide variety of methods, including Neuro-Linguistic Programming (NLP), to speed up the process. We will address our thoughts that influence behaviors and the behaviors that influence our thoughts. We will develop a better understanding of how your brain processes and stores information and gain the ability to view your emotions, actions, and outcomes as something you have power over.

Inner child work has helped many on their journey to heal their inner wounds and reparent the child within. I am one such testament to its results. After pursuing my healing, I decided to devote myself to helping others with this type of healing. I know what this work has done for me and my life. I'm positive it will help you create a life where you have control over your emotions, reactions, and outcomes. I hope to share this empowerment with everyone who picks up this book.

INTRODUCTION

Imagine a future where the adult you are in control of and your inner child help keep you grounded and full of wonder. You will make peace with parts of your past and discover how to work to become the best version of yourself.

A word of caution before you start. Knowledge will only get you so far. Real change comes as action. This book is best thought of as an action book. Do the exercises. Do the work. And you will make positive strides toward creating the life you've always wanted. Your inner peace begins now. I'm excited to join you on this journey.

1
HAVEN OF HEALING

The wound is not my fault, but the healing is my responsibility.

— MARIANNE WILLIAMSON

Have you ever walked around your neighborhood and smelled something delicious cooking? Something so sweet to your nose that you instantly go back in time to a pleasant memory? Maybe baking cookies with your grandma or a backyard barbeque with your dad. There's something about the smell of food that can take us back to a moment in time.

Our body experiences things through all five senses. Memories, specifically, are stored using sensory data. That's why when you smell something, it can trigger a memory. Or when you touch something, like a soft teddy bear, it can bring you back to when you got a favorite stuffed animal.

Not all sensory experiences bring up pleasant memories. For example, you may have some negative thoughts and feelings around a school bell. This year, my son and I went to his school's "mock class" the day before school started. It's where we could walk the halls so he could learn where his classrooms were and meet his teachers for the year. It was a wonderful bonding moment as we cracked jokes and talked about what he expects from his classes.

But the moment the bell rang, I was instantly taken back to my school years. My heartbeat raced with the feeling that I was on the clock rushing to get to my next class. And that sinking feeling you may have gotten every so often that you didn't finish high school. Does that happen to anyone else, or is it just me? Anyway, all it took was one sound to rip me out of being present for my boy and back into the feeling of being a kid in school again. And if I'm being honest with myself, I acted like it, too. I rushed from one room to the next, sitting in the back of the class and whispering to my son even as the teachers did their best to keep our attention on details for the upcoming year.

If sounds, smells, and other sensory experiences can unwillingly invoke such powerful actions, it makes sense that we can tap into our environment to create a feeling we desire. When working with our inner child, we want to create a space filled with calm, safety, and security, especially as we dive into overwhelming feelings and emotions.

This space can help you decompress from the stressors of the world and be the perfect place to help you feel balanced. When you and your surroundings are calm, you have a better chance of reconnecting and rebuilding your relationship with your inner child.

PREPARING YOUR PHYSICAL SANCTUARY

Your physical space can be a simple corner in your house where you have a place to sit and take a breath. It doesn't need to be anything fancy. Even your favorite chair can constitute the perfect 'safe' space for you to relax if your mind, body, and soul feel at peace when you are there.

As you create your physical space, keep a few things in mind. For starters, you want it to be somewhere where you have a certain amount of privacy. Some exercises mentioned in this book can bring up different emotions, and a little privacy can help you complete the exercise without interruptions or wandering eyes. It helps if your space has a little room on the floor as well. There are a few exercises that require some floor space, even if it's just a few feet. Personally, I have a space where I can close the door. This helps minimize distractions and lets my family know that I need a little me time. However, any space in your home will do.

You also want to consider what does and doesn't make sense in your space. You want to make room for what serves you and get rid of the rest. Pictures of your loved ones may spark love and peace, but a giant pile of bills will most likely only bring more stress. Some people like to bring in plants and curtains, and others like crystals and candles. The beauty of creating this kind of space is it should help to represent you, and it should elicit a feeling of safety, security, and calm.

If possible, keep electronics out of this space. Personally, when I disconnect from the world and take a step away from my phone, computer, and TV, I feel more at peace. Try it and see if it works for you, too.

Now that we've got your physical space set up, let's move on to another very important space we need to create.

BUILDING YOUR MENTAL SPACE

Much of the real work happens in your subconscious. So we need to create a comfortable place in our mind that we can easily access. Unlike our physical space, anywhere we can imagine is available to us in our minds. Your brain has a wonderful ability to design a place where you feel calm and relaxed, safe and secure, warm and happy—even if you've never been there before. The options are endless.

Before you begin, let's brainstorm some ideas. Where do you feel most at peace? Is it in nature? A forest or a beach? Do you feel most at peace indoors? A big, comfy lounge with tall bookshelves and a Papa San chair? Anywhere or anything you can imagine, you can create in your mind.

Take some time to go through pictures and images, identify what places make you feel something, and set those aside. Don't limit yourself to what you consider. It can be somewhere you've been before or somewhere you would love to go. It can be a real place, a fictional world, or something in-between. The goal is to give yourself options and ideas on what makes you feel comfortable and can create a sense of calm.

As you set your pictures and images aside, ask yourself what it is about that picture you like. Is it the way the trees let the light through to the ground floor? Is it a giant wrap-around porch with a rocking chair? A specific set of curtains or paint scheme you liked? These elements can create your perfect mental space. The goal is to create a space that's unique to you and exactly the way you want it to be.

Once you know what type of place brings you comfort, it's time to create your mental space. Start in a comfortable position. We're going to daydream for a moment, so you can do this with your eyes open or closed. Imagine an empty room. This is a magic room. You can create anything you want inside it. It's big enough to hold what you want and just the right size to make you feel comfortable.

Fill this room with the things you want in your space. If your perfect space is outdoors, you can fill the room with your outdoor scene. What do you see on the floor or ground below you? Carpet? Sand? Grass? Blankets? Are there walls? Can you see the ocean? What colors do you see? If you don't see color, what would you add? What sounds do you hear? If you hear nothing, what sound would you want? The more detail you add to your room, the better. The more you can involve all five senses, the more real this room will feel.

Once you've created your room, it's time to take a breath and get comfortable in your new space. While you're here, let's check-in with how it makes your body feel. You may feel joy, peace, or any range of emotions. You can also feel nothing. This is ok. The point is to note how you feel all over while you're in your room. Notice any tingling or tightness in your body.

If you feel anything that isn't quite right or feels uncomfortable, change it. When I first went about creating my mental room, I added too many things. Rugs, plants, chairs, instruments, bookshelves, the list goes on and on. I thought it was comfy as I was putting all the pieces together. However, the opposite turned out to be true. When I took a moment to enjoy my room, something felt off about it. My chest was noticeably tighter, and my body was very tense in my mind when I "stepped" into this room. Little by little, I adjusted and removed pieces. I changed the color of the walls and took out some instruments until the feelings in my body went away.

This mental safe space is a resource you now have access to at any time. You can add or change things as you see fit. Don't feel you're stuck with your original idea. The goal is to create a mental place you go before, sometimes during, and even after any inner child work. It helps to ground you and can even give you a place to relax and destress from whatever life throws your way.

You may think, "but I don't 'see' anything." All I see is black static when I close my eyes. Don't worry. That's normal for some people, and it's exactly where I started the first time I tried. As with any new skill, it takes practice, and the more you do this exercise and visit your room, the easier it will get.

Remember that your safe place will not resemble someone else's. Much like fingerprints, these environments are completely unique to us. While you might feel at peace in the forest, someone else might find more solace in a library. Whatever you create is exactly the right place for you.

Now that we have created your perfect place in your mind, let me show you how to access it instantly at any time.

HOW TO CREATE AN ANCHOR POINT

Anchoring is a powerful tool that creates a "button" you can push to have near-instant access to a resource in your body[17], like the mental room we just created. An anchor is simply a physical touch point you set on your body that accesses the resource you attach to the point. It can be anything from emotions, behaviors, reminders, and memories, to name a few things.

You've most likely created anchors in your life without realizing it already. Maybe you have a favorite gift from your dad that sparks an instant memory recall or a particular outfit you wear that makes you feel powerful, confident, and ready to take on the

HEALING YOUR INNER CHILD

world. These are examples of anchoring to an object. We're going to set anchors on your body that you can activate whenever and wherever you want.

There are five simple steps with anchoring.

First, determine what you want to anchor. For this exercise, let's use the mental room you just created.

Next, remember your room. Put yourself in the middle of your room. See your room, hear your room, feel the feelings of your room. Fully experience the way your room makes you and your body feel.

You should notice a difference in your body when you've entered your room. You may be in a relaxed state and feel calm. This is exactly what you want, as we created this room to help you feel this way.

Now, choose a place on your body to 'anchor' this room. It should be a place that is not easily bumped into your daily life. Personally, I like to touch my thumb and pinky finger on my non-dominant hand for my room.

Once you've chosen your anchor, it's time to set it. While you're in the room, in your mind and feel your body relaxed and calm, touch your anchor point and hold it for five seconds, then release.

Congratulations, you've intentionally set your first anchor.

The last step is to test your anchor. If you use your thumb and pinky finger as your anchor point, shake your hands a little to release any tension you may have. Give your body a little wiggle to wake it up.

Now that you're not actively in your mental room, touch your anchor point in the same way you set the anchor. You should immediately feel your body returning to its relaxed and calm state, and your room should flash into your mind.

Don't resist the anchor. Let it do what you've set it to do. Allow it to adjust your mental state.

Anchors are temporary by design. If you don't continue to push your anchor, it will eventually disappear. To make your mental room anchor permanent, you need to push it often. The more you push it, the better and stronger its connection to your mental room will be.

Remember when I said you can anchor any resource you want instant access to? You can set as many anchors as you can remember. The more you activate them, the stronger they get. Having instant access to resources like confidence, joy, courage, and curiosity goes a long way when doing inner child work and with life.

FINDING YOUR PEACE

Everything you read in this book is a process. Every step you take toward healing and reparenting is a step forward. While progress might not always seem immediately clear, you are taking the right steps and making progress.

Creating a safe space to engage in your inner child's work is an important part of the process. It's hard to work on yourself and heal your inner child if your body is feeling out of control and stressed. Now that we know how to create a relaxing environment, it's time to invite your inner child out to play.

2

MEETING YOUR INNER CHILD

The voice I finally heard that day was my own—the girl I'd locked away at ten years old, the girl I was before the world told me who to be—and she said: Here I am. I'm taking over now.

— GLENNON DOYLE

Nicole is in her late twenties, struggling with her marriage and fighting against people-pleasing tendencies. Feeling lost in her day-to-day life, she notices her responses don't always match how she's feeling. She snapped at her husband because he didn't fold the socks correctly. She belittled a coworker at a meeting because they didn't know the acronym for the project they were working on. A red light that seemed a little long puts her in a bad mood. At the end of each day, she is drained and exhausted. She can't figure out what's really causing her perpetual mood swings and inappropriate responses.

Finally fed up, she reached out to me to talk. Nicole shared all about the little things that trigger big responses and how she feels out of control of her emotions and reactions. Picking one of her reactions, I asked her to think of the earliest memory she had when she had that kind of response.

To Nicole's surprise, she was about eight years old. She remembers the moment so clearly. Her mother was teaching her how to fold her laundry and made her feel like she wasn't good enough. "No, no, no. Not like that. Like this." She heard her mother's voice repeatedly every time she tried. "Are you listening to me? Why can't you get it right?" As Nicole went deeper into her memory, I could see her shrink in her seat. She was reliving the moment with her mother.

I asked Nicole, who was in this child-like state, what she needed at that moment. What did she need to help her get through this experience? Her answer? *Patience, understanding, a friendly voice, and a hug.*

This was the first time Nicole intentionally interacted with her child self. It was the first time she was introduced to a part of her that was unconsciously running her life. It was also the first time she realized she could reparent (give her child self what she needs) the situation and help her heal and move on.

Nicole has since strengthened her marriage and has developed firm boundaries to counteract her people-pleasing and exaggerated response tendencies. She told me that our talk had been an eye-opening experience. She had never realized that there was a part of her that still felt the pain of childhood.

The game-changer was her realizing that she could support herself now, where her parents hadn't been able to in the past. Showing up for herself in the way her inner child needed gave her a better sense of control and peace.

You and Nicole are similar. Your experience may have been different, but the lingering memories and wounds from your childhood are creating some unhealthy responses for you as an adult. Just like Nicole, you can meet and heal your inner child.

WHAT *IS* THE INNER CHILD?

Your inner child is a part of you that has been present since your birth. It remembers and holds on to the experiences of your past, both the positive and negative moments. It lives in your subconscious and often is the trigger for certain behaviors or responses. Your inner child is key to who you are, and it's a vital piece of who you want to be[1].

Much like the name suggests, your inner child is a direct connection to your childhood and sometimes takes control over your conscious responses, which can cause trouble for you as an adult. Can you imagine what your day would look like if you let an 8-year-old make all the decisions for you? You may start out with a trip to the ice cream store and then have a silly response to your boss's email, followed by a mild tantrum stuck in traffic. You'd probably round the day out with a trip to the trampoline park. Sure, a day like that might sound fun, and it certainly can be. But if every day is like that, you can probably imagine how your adult life would go.

Everyone has an inner child. It's one way we learn and grow. It holds meaning, messages, emotions, beliefs, and memories of your past. This is also the part of you that has hopes and dreams for your future. As you may have guessed, your inner child can have a lot of input into how you react to the world around you. It can be playful and fun, and it also bears the burdens of troubling childhood experiences.

For example, if we experience disappointment, neglect, or even trauma in our early days, our inner child internalizes those wounds. When left untreated, the wounds of our childhood become the foundation for triggers as an adult.

Our inner child often takes a backseat, allowing us to go about our day. That is, until they experience something they don't like. Much like the child in the grocery store who didn't get their treat, that's when they try to reach out and get our attention. It's up to you to listen to what they might need. Perhaps they feel lonely, or maybe they feel unheard. Whatever that wound is, it likely comes out in your life through bouts of feeling out of control. Recognizing when your inner child is trying to get your attention is a critical step in the healing process.

Renowned psychiatrist Carl Jung rejected the idea that we come into this world as a blank slate. Instead, he favored the thought that we all have an archetype of a child within our subconscious. He believed there were different manifestations of a collective consciousness—referred to now as Inner Child Archetypes—that reached their potential with conscious action. In non-psychiatric speech, Jung was the first person to believe that our subconscious inner child could affect our conscious actions[9].

To better understand your inner child, it's important to know what archetype is running the show. Read the descriptions below and see which ones seem relevant to your experiences. Don't force relevance. As you work through these pages, you'll get the tools you need to heal and change your archetype to something that better suits who you want to be.

THE SEVEN INNER CHILD ARCHETYPES

You may have heard the phrase wounded, shadow, or dark side used for these archetypes. They are interchangeable terms for the same thing. For this book, I'll use the term shadow to reference the negative elements of the archetypes to eliminate any confusion with the specific Wounded Child archetype.

The Wounded Child

This inner child has experienced a tragic or harsh upbringing, usually involving psychological or physical abuse in the past. They often bring this experience into adulthood with reactionary and untrusting behavior. This archetype can feel neglected and can be detrimental to relationships. Those with a wounded inner child are at a higher risk of being abusive themselves, making healing and reparenting vital.

The wounded child is one that can have immense compassion when it is healed. Through embracing and harmonizing this archetype, you might discover renewed compassion for yourself and others who have suffered abuse. A healed, wounded child brings a certain mercy and brightness to their everyday lives and becomes a haven for others who experience childhood tragedies.

The Orphaned Child

The orphaned child often shows up with an intense emphasis on personal independence. This archetype occurs from loneliness and emotional neglect in the early years. They are desperate to avoid future wounds and often lash out when they feel rejected. They isolate and draw away from interactions with others, including well-meaning check-ins from loved ones.

When healed, the orphaned child can easily stand on their own. They are independent when needed and accept help with grace. They create their own inner reality and intuition from their experience.

The Magical Child

The magical child can see magic and miracles every day. To them, nothing is impossible, as they see the energy that connects us all. This archetype is highly intuitive, with a strong sense of will. They challenge the status quo and question everything.

A shadow magical child was scorned or dismissed when they would daydream and create imaginary fantasies. This leads to disillusionment and a loss of belief in miracles. A wounded magical child causes depression and anxiety when they lose hope of accomplishing their dreams.

The Nature Child

The natural child is one who has a deep connection with the Earth and nature. They feel most at home outdoors and will often spend a lot of time with plants and animals. They might even have an intuitive connection with them, able to identify and communicate their needs to others. The natural child may also be seen collecting rocks, feathers, twigs, and other treasures they found on the earth.

A shadowy nature child is prone to mistreating others. Their connection with nature is severed, and their respect for living things is torn. They may abuse or neglect nature, animals, or even themselves.

The Eternal Child

The eternal child is more free-spirited and carefree than most. They enjoy simple pleasures and keep their childlike wonder. They have an unbridled enthusiasm that doesn't wane as they age. They can see things differently than others, which makes them great problem solvers.

A shadow eternal child avoids responsibility and refuses to grow up. They can reject social norms, shy away from the rules of the real world, and become overly dependent on someone else to take care of them.

The Needy Child

This archetype shares some similarities with the wounded and orphaned child. The needy child seeks to find what they are missing. It comes from neglect, though they may not know what that neglect was. A needy child is constantly searching for something and is never content. They may spend their entire lives searching and never find what they are looking for. They have a strong sense of fairness and justice and pursue it with passion.

A shadowy child may be self-centered, self-absorbed, and oblivious to what others around them need. They focus on themselves and only do things for others when they get a benefit out of it.

The Divine Child

The divine child has a distinct link to the divine and holds on to purity and innocence. They believe in atonement and have deep ties to their spiritual side. This might look like religious beliefs or an ability to commune with the energy of the world around them. Someone with a divine inner child might come across as mysterious and fantastical or may be sought after for healing and divine direction.

A shadow divine child may be a guru or leader who harms their followers. They often rely on deception and domination and are easily angered and lose control when they are confronted[31].

HOW TO SPOT YOUR SHADOW

Everyone has the opportunity for their shadow archetype to show. So, it's helpful to know how to recognize it. The first step is to notice what resonated with you as you read the descriptions above. Either the shadow side or the positive side of the archetype may spark an emotion or a reaction in you. This is a sign from your archetype. It's possible that you may connect with more than one of the inner child types. That's okay. Work with the one that most closely resonates with you. This will help you better understand how to address your shadow side and heal.

If you are a natural child and notice some unhealthy responses in your life, take some time in nature. Pick up some leaves, rocks, or feathers. Speak to the flowers and surround yourself with life. While this won't eliminate your triggers, it can help ground you and create a healthy connection with your inner child.

Your inner child typically develops its shadow through some type of emotional struggle as a child. While this might be something as obvious as abuse, for many of us, we don't need a traumatic event to create these wounds. It could be something as simple as not getting the exact type of emotional support you need in the moment that creates a wound for you.

If you had a rough time learning something new, you may have needed encouragement, but you received sympathy instead. This mismatch of emotional needs can create a lasting effect on your confidence when you try new things in the future.

Some potential reasons you might be dealing with a shadow inner child are:

- emotional neglect
- feeling unheard as a child
- parents or other adults discouraging your innate abilities
- feeling a lack of control, such as moving all the time or divorce between parents
- psychological, physical, or sexual abuse
- unmet expectations
- needing a hug or encouragement that you never received
- becoming an adult before finishing out your childhood

As you work to recognize your inner child, there are a few questions you can answer to help bring more awareness to some shadow tendencies. Do you constantly apologize for everything? Do you feel you are always at fault when something goes wrong? Do you struggle with constant feelings of guilt? Do you overreact to situations and blow your emotions out of proportion? Do you snap at others for what feels like no reason? Do you have triggers that elicit negative emotions? Do you feel the need to give in and please others, even if you don't want to?

If we know these triggers resulted from experiences when we were children, why didn't our parents know how to help us the way we needed? Well, it's because our needs as children differed from those of our parents, friends, and other adults in our lives. This is obviously different when talking about abuse. Abuse is never acceptable, and there is no excuse for it.

Children make mistakes. It's part of growing up. If the mistake is one that requires correction from an adult, these corrections may make us feel uncomfortable. After all, we experienced correction as a child. Our parents may have been trying to mold and shape our behavior and help us learn a better way to do something. However, the way they went about it differed from what we needed. They are not mind readers, and as children, we may not have been capable of saying or even being aware of what we needed to help us through.

My youngest child has daily chores. Most days, he does them well. However, some days, he skips a few details because he wants to play instead of work. Honestly, I don't blame him. I'm not a huge fan of chores, either. But they must be done. His chore is the bathroom. This entails cleaning the sink, mirror, toilet, and floor, taking out the trash, and restocking supplies. A simple wipe-down is good enough because it's done every day. For a few days in a row, he didn't sweep the floor or take out the trash. So, I did a spot check after he said he was done. I pointed out the pieces he missed and asked what was so important that he skipped this part of his chore. He broke into tears and got mad because I was "so strict."

While this interaction wasn't an intentional mismatch of emotional needs, he may need something different in this situation than I can provide for him. Not because I don't want to, but because he can't tell me what he needs, or he may not even know what he needs. He's only ten. He may not realize what he needs at that moment until he's an adult and has the words and worldly experience to know what he is missing. And while I can't say for certain, this interaction may later turn into his own inner child issue that shows up in his adult life.

NEGLECT AND YOUR INNER CHILD

Neglect is another way we develop wounds and bring out our shadow child. Not all neglect is intentional, and some happen because of circumstances beyond control. Instead of blaming and being chained to these situations, neglect shows us where and how we can show up for ourselves now to help heal.

Neglect takes two primary forms: physical and emotional.

- **Physical neglect** occurs when a child's physical needs are not being met. This might mean that the child experiences food insecurity or inconsistent housing. While this type of neglect typically means that there is a pattern of these inconsistencies, it can also take as little as one majorly emotional event at a vulnerable time in our childhood to create a shadow child.
- **Emotional neglect** occurs when a child is not having their emotional needs met. This is unique to a situation, but it often involves failing to form secure, positive bonds with adult figures or other children. This type of neglect can occur for many reasons, such as your parents being busy or struggling with their own issues and unable to help you with your emotional needs.

INTRODUCE YOURSELF TO YOURSELF

We've been introduced to our inner child and have a better understanding of why they hang around and act the way they do. Now, we need to reconnect with them and re-introduce ourselves to our subconscious selves.

Before we dive into some of our memories and experiences, we need to remember that children (and your inner child) connect best with play. Do you remember being on the playground as a kid, meeting some other children, and leaving as "friends" after a few minutes? That's exactly what we're going to do to get started with our child self.

Here are some ways to introduce yourself to your inner child.

1. **Get out and play!** Indulge in some good old-fashioned child-like fun. Jump in a puddle, sing your favorite song at the top of your lungs, blow bubbles in your backyard, play the floor is lava, the list is endless. For a list of play resources visit www.vitalskillspress.com/innerchild-resources.
2. **Stretch those creative muscles.** There is a reason that younger grades in school have a lot of activities that include crafts or drawing. Children learn better through creative expression! So, grab a blank piece of paper and start drawing whatever comes to mind. The more creative, the better. A spaceship beaming up ice cream to feed a 12-eyed dog-cow pet is just one example of the creativity of a child.
3. **Color.** Grab a coloring book and a box of crayons, and pick a page. This is best done with a physical coloring book, not an app on your phone. Head to your favorite bookstore, go to the children's book section, and pick one that interests you. You'd be amazed at the range of subjects coloring books come in. And don't worry, you can still color outside the lines if you'd like.

Playing is fun, and it sparks a change in how you think. You want to see the world through the eyes of a child. This requires getting back into the mindset of a child. You can start by asking yourself a few simple questions:

- *What makes me happy?*
- *How can I live in the moment?*
- *How can I let go of control?*

Embrace what makes you happy. This brings out your joyful side and lets you tap into a childlike wonder. Living in the moment can be difficult as an adult. We've been conditioned over the years to conform, to follow the rules, and to be in control. But this wasn't how we operated as a child. Most children don't think too far beyond the moment they are in. They don't have deadlines at work, they don't have bills to pay, and they don't have the weight of adult responsibilities.

Now, I'm not asking you to give up everything and go live a carefree life. Take baby steps to release control. Dance under the stars at first, and then move onto something silly, like blurting out your favorite song on the subway or running freely through the park. It's okay to let loose occasionally and reconnect with childhood. The best way to meet your inner child is to give them an avenue to come out. What better way than to tap into childlike play?

EMBRACE YOUR INNER CHILD

For some of us, childhood was a long time ago, so it makes sense that we may or may not remember what we were like as a child. So, let's take a moment and get to know our child self a little better.

These next few exercises are perfect for the space we created in the last chapter. Grab a seat and take a moment to relax. You can even enter the space you created in your mind to help you relax and wind down.

Exercise: Asking Your Inner Child to Reveal Themselves

One of my favorite ways to speak to my inner child is to ask if that part of me will talk. If you've ever said something like, "There's a part of me that wants to do this, but another part wants to do something else," you already got the basic idea.

Your inner child is a part of you. They are not the whole of you, just a portion. So, let's see if they're willing to identify themself. Right now, all we're going to do is connect with this part. It's the first step to conflict resolution, which we will get into in a later chapter.

All the exercises in this book can be done with any gender. Fill in your pronouns where applicable.

In a comfortable chair and relaxed state, they said, "There's a part of me that's childlike. [He/She/They] has/have been with me my whole life. Is [he/she/they] willing to identify [herself/himself/themself]?"

Pay close attention to your body. Once you've asked your childlike self to identify themself, you may feel a tingling somewhere. Or it may feel like pressure or a slight change in temperature. It will be a feeling. Notice it.

Once you feel it, recognize your childlike self for identifying themselves. You can say something like, "Thank you for identifying yourself. It's nice to meet you."

For now, all we're working on is the habit of identifying and speaking with the different "parts" of us.

If you felt nothing, that's okay. This exercise may take more than one try before your inner child reveals themselves. You may need to have a play session or lean into relaxation a little more before your inner child will come out to play.

Thank your inner child for their willingness to take part—even if they didn't show up for you. The best way to create rapport with your parts is to be respectful of them. After all, they've gotten you this far in life.

Once you've finished this exercise, you can take a moment and shake your body to let loose a little and grab a glass of water. It's both good for your body and a great way to signal to yourself that the work you just did is over.

Exercise: Tell Me About Yourself

Taking the time to get to *know* your inner child is vital to the process. And what better way to get to know yourself than with journaling? Pick one of the following prompts and explore how you would answer them as a child. You can mix these up or create your own prompts. The goal is to remember what you liked when you were younger.

- As a kid, I used to daydream about…
- My favorite activity when I was home for the summer was…
- My best friend and I used to play…
- When I was seven, I used to wonder about…

Don't overthink it! Remember that *being* a child often meant being simple. Sometimes, simple answers are the best ones. You probably didn't have a huge story about what you did over the summer when you were ten. Let yourself go when you write these journal entries. Don't stop your pen to give your answers much thought. Just write whatever comes to you.

Now that you have found your inner child and begun interacting with them, it's time to free them. They have probably felt locked up and ignored for a while, and that's partly why they act out in unhelpful and sometimes detrimental ways. Giving them the space and freedom to express themselves is one of the best things you can do for yourself.

3
FREE YOUR PLAYFUL SOUL

The cry we hear from deep in our hearts comes from the wounded child within. Healing this inner child's pain is the key to transforming anger, sadness, and fear.

— THICH NHAT HAHN

IS YOUR INNER CHILD RUNNING YOUR ADULTHOOD?

Heather was an emotional wreck. Her tears were never far from view, which is embarrassing at any age, but when you're in your late 40s and can cry at the drop of a hat, it's downright devastating. Her local coffee shop got her order wrong, and that sent her into a tear-filled breakdown at the counter because she wanted vanilla spice, not pumpkin. When her best friend posted a picture on social media having fun without her, she would melt into a pool of sobs.

It may come as no surprise that Heather's life wasn't run by her adult self. If anything didn't go her way, she immediately burst into a full-blown toddler-style tantrum, complete with foot stomps and fists.

When Heather discussed this with me, I asked her who she thought was running her life. She felt like a trapped child who couldn't get out. She felt small, unheard, and lost in a world that required her to ramp up drama just to be noticed. She felt seven, back in her childhood home, surrounded by her brothers. Her mother wasn't very attentive, and her father wasn't in the picture anymore. The only thing she could do to get her mother's attention was to act out and cause a scene.

Those impressionable years set the tone for nearly everything Heather did in life. She lived by the motto, "The squeaky wheel gets the grease." To be fair, it often worked and got her what she wanted. However, this behavior also backfired. It ruined her relationships and a few marriages, and even her best friend couldn't stay around anymore.

You may not have extreme moments like these, but if you take a moment to step back and think, you may remember moments when your inner child took the wheel and reacted. Your inner child might show up in ways you may not even be aware of. Like any child, yours wants to be seen and acknowledged. If they don't get what they want, they act out to get you to take notice. Relationships are one of those areas that can be deeply impacted by your shadow wounds.

The Inner Child and Relationships

As a group, humans are a social species and rely on one another. It's why we formed tribes, then villages, towns, and cities. So, the art of getting along with the people is a key part of not just daily life but survival. When your shadow inner child is running the show, they can show up in a variety of ways.

Lack of Boundaries

Have you ever met someone who will tell you their life story the moment you meet them? The gory details of their latest medical issues? The strained relationship they have with their neighbor? It's exhausting to listen to and a little uncomfortable if you don't even know their name. This is a sign of an inner child that doesn't know boundaries.

Another way a lack of boundaries shows up in our lives is when we allow people to treat us in a way we don't want to be treated. Maybe they raise their voice, talk over you, or worse, put their hands on you when you don't want them to.

Lack of boundaries doesn't have to be intentional or abusive. Some people who disrespect your boundaries have poor boundaries themselves. Which means they may or may not even know that something is—or even can be—a boundary.

Maintaining and respecting boundaries creates healthy relationships. If you cannot stay firm in what you allow, or you cannot respect someone else's boundaries, you set yourself up for trouble.

Jealousy

Jealousy and envy go hand-in-hand. If you fear what others are doing or fiercely hold on to your possessions and covet someone else's things, it's a big sign your inner child is running the show. It's okay to want and desire things, but when taken to the extreme, jealousy can destroy any relationship.

Staying in Unhealthy Relationships

People who stay in abusive relationships usually have unmet and unhealed wounds[12]. They often find themselves in a relationship that mirrors one from their childhood. This may be because it is their only reference to what a relationship should be.

This concept also goes beyond abuse as well. A relationship that doesn't allow you to be yourself, for whatever reason, can be unhealthy. Feeling like you must hide something from your partner, the need to walk on eggshells around them, feeling trapped but unable to put your finger on why, and so many other scenarios can all be signs of an unhealthy relationship.

Another telltale sign of an unhealthy relationship is settling for "the devil, you know." This means staying with someone because you're afraid of what it's like on the other side. Not wanting to be lonely or needing to be with someone, even if it's wrong, are all symptoms of wounds you should address.

To work on these parts of yourself, you first need to know where your inner child is showing up in your relationship. Begin the process by noticing when something doesn't feel right. Then, try to name what you're feeling. If you want to write this down in a journal, you can see patterns where it shows up in your life. In very few instances, one time is not a pattern or something you should be concerned with. We all have off days and down days. We're all human, and no one is perfect.

Once you notice a pattern of feelings, acknowledge what you feel. Don't accept it just yet because the next step is to challenge what you feel. I don't mean to discredit it or invalidate it. Ask yourself if what you feel really belongs to you. Or is it a feeling or reaction from something or someone else?

Again, right now, we're just noticing, naming, and checking in with these feelings to make sure they really belong to us. You should do this with grace and love for yourself. Your feelings are valid and real. This step in the process is to question gently if they are yours to keep and deal with or if you can let them go.

No matter what you work through in this step, I am not advocating for making immediate and rash changes if you believe your inner child is ruining your relationship. If you are in an abusive relationship, please seek help. If you are in a relationship where you see patterns of your inner child running your life, seek a professional to support your healing process.

Is there a time when your inner child can support and enhance your relationships? Absolutely! When two people with healthy boundaries, trust, and a sense of wonder come together, they can experience what relationships are meant to be.

The Inner Child in the Workplace

Whether you are an executive of a big firm, a stay-at-home parent, or anything in between, the pressure can often make your shadow inner child show up. This can cause additional stress and create a working environment we want to avoid. However, if you are aware of a few workplace signs that your inner child is in charge, it can go a long way to making your work life more enjoyable.

- **Overly Sensitive to Criticism:** Everyone has room to improve. Even the boss. If you have a hard time receiving criticism, this can be a sign your inner child needs some soothing. There is a difference between constructive criticism, designed to help you grow and succeed in what you do, and criticism that puts you down or keeps you in your place. You should react differently to constructive criticism than when someone uses criticism to demotivate you.

- **People Pleaser:** If you take on more than you can handle, going above and beyond your duties even if you don't want to, or saying yes to things when you want to say no, you might be in a people-pleasing cycle. It's ok to be a valued member of a team and to do work you're proud of. But when that happens at the expense of you, your boundaries, and your sense of self-worth, it's not ok.
- **Overwhelm and Burn Out:** This often happens because you are taking on more than you should be. It's okay to say "no" when you need to. It's also okay to take time away from work. Someone who is a workaholic or ignores their body telling them to rest may be dealing with an inner child who was never good enough. If you feel compelled to overwork and you don't know why, you may want to dive into what's causing the drive. As with everything, there are times when putting your head down and getting the job done is necessary. I can honestly say that while writing this book, I've spent a few long hours in my office, but this isn't the norm for me. I don't work excessive hours to the point of burnout for long periods of time. Sprints and defined projects happen. For this, we're talking about chronic overwhelm and burn out.

In the game of life, nothing is truly cut and dry. Sometimes, it's appropriate to be an adult and step up to get the job done. Some people choose to work the hours they do because they get a sense of joy and satisfaction from it. If it charges you up, then by all means, keep doing it. However, if you work to avoid something, or it doesn't feel good, see what's at the root of the issue.

THE HEALING JOURNEY

So far, we've laid the groundwork for recognizing how your inner child is showing up in your life. We've created a safe space for reconnecting and have even started intentionally eliciting your inner child. Next, we start the process of healing.

Why is Healing the Inner Child Important?

The simple answer is that your inner child is a part of you. You wouldn't leave any visible wound, like a cut or broken bone, untreated, and the same goes for your inner wounds and shadow child. To give you the best chance at becoming who you are meant to be, you need to address all the areas of your life that don't serve you or help you become your best self.

When you confront the wounds of your past, you realize there is a whole other side of you that's been waiting for your attention. It is one reason you don't have everything you want in life because there is a part of you that still needs your help and your guidance to heal.

When I was a little girl, Saturday mornings were the time to clean our room and watch cartoons. If it was nice out, my mother would kick us outside once the rooms were to her liking. I knew what she expected. But there's one particular Saturday that really stands out to me and has had quite an impact on my life, even today.

That morning, I surveyed my work. My room is decent; all my things were picked up off the floor. Vacuumed? Check. The closet is mostly orderly, and the clutter is gone. Check. Bed made? Check. Desk organized? Check. I tell my mother I'm done. "No, it's not. Go back and do it again." Okay. Yeah, I know I need to pick up my dirty clothes basket and take it to the laundry room. Oh, and I need to clean up the piles of paper on my desk. Shoot, I also forgot to dust. So, let me knock that out real quick. Time to grab my mom and have her check. She walked into my room, said, "Nope," and walked right back out. Hmmm. What did I miss? Ok, let's straighten up under the bed and do a better job dusting. "I'm ready, mom." Again, she walked in and said, "Nope."

"What am I missing? I've done everything!"

"Nope!" was all the response I got.

Okay. Move more things around on my desk. Adjust my bed sheets. Tuck the boxes under my bed a little further. Make sure nothing is on the floor. Stand in the doorway and scan, trying desperately to figure out what's been missed. I've got nothing more. "Can you check now, mom?" Again, she walks in, "Nope, you know what I want," and walks out.

I still do not know what it could be. I know; let's grab Dad; maybe he knows. Dad walks in, says, "I don't know what your mother is looking for," and walks out. Great. Now what? So, I sit on my bed and wait. Five minutes. Ten minutes. 15. I just sat there. Then I called my mom for another look.

"It's good. You can go outside now."

Are you kidding me? I hadn't done anything since the last time she looked! What in the world did I do?

My mom meant well, and she had a lot on her plate. She raised four kids, and practically half the neighborhood was at our house most days. So, she was busy. But I couldn't figure this one out. Other than cleaning as a chore designed to waste time and give my mother a break. *(To be fair, since then, I've talked with my mother about this, and she can't tell me what was going on for her at that moment either.)*

To this day, my room wouldn't pass my mother's inspection, and I have piles of clothes and other things lying around. I haven't dusted in forever. I learned that cleaning was a way to give her a break.

Today, when dealing with my kids, I do my best to tell them what they missed. Because I remember how frustrating this was for me, so it's not the worst-case scenario that came from this experience. But that old wound is still there, and it shows up in my life in different ways.

Inner child work is a healing process. While healing is its own great destination, it's important to realize that healing can feel empowering! As you work through this process, you are no longer at the mercy of your emotions. You confront them head-on, make informed decisions, and start living like the adult you want to be.

The Five Steps to Healing Your Inner Child

This process is simple, but it's not always easy. We've already started on this journey together, and I'll lay out all the steps for you so you'll know what's coming up. Don't rush through each step. Give each one the time and attention you need. That's what will create the most lasting changes in your life. Each step may take a different amount of time for each situation you work through. That's normal.

While some emotions may surface during the process, acknowledge them and remember to be kind to yourself. As a reminder, if you need to do this for a difficult time in your life, I strongly suggest working with a qualified professional.

1. **Acknowledge the Inner Child:** The first step is always to acknowledge what's going on. We started this step in the last chapter, and we will build on it going forward. Some exercises in later chapters will help you identify when your inner child kept a memory of an event and how old that part is.
2. **Validate What Happened:** You may have grown used to sweeping uncomfortable emotions and events under the rug. We all do it from time to time. However, this isn't a healthy way to live. Those unaddressed emotions bubble up in other ways through our actions and behavior patterns. Acknowledge whatever pain might be in your past. Recognize that it happened, and validate your thoughts, feelings, and emotions surrounding the event.
3. **Identify What You Needed:** No matter what event you work through, this step is to identify what was missing for you at the moment. Was it a hug? Encouragement? A hand to hold on to? Someone to guide you? Someone to protect you? Whatever it was, as the adult you are now, you can work with your inner child to identify what you need to help you through.
4. **Be There For YOU:** Once you know what you need, give it to yourself. Remind your inner child that you made it through this situation. You are older now, and

you're there to help her. You work together to safely navigate the situation. We can't change what happened to us in the past. We can, however, be there for our inner child and help *them* through the situation they keep holding on to.

5. **Step Into The Future:** There's a 100% chance you'll encounter a similar situation in the future. The last step of healing is to 'test' the changes in your controlled environment. With the power of you and your inner child working together from the last step, imagine a scenario in the future where you might experience the situation again and notice how you work in harmony to get the best result as the person you want to be.

As you reconnect, you might be unfamiliar with the needs of your inner child, or it might feel strange to keep those needs in mind. It's okay. As you work through this process, schedule regular check-ins with yourself. Taking care of you while you're healing is vital. We'll go into more detail on this in a later chapter. For now, start small. A simple internal check over your morning coffee or a journal you write in before you go to bed are two effective ways to keep on top of what your body is telling you.

HEALING THROUGH SELF-ACCEPTANCE

Nothing bothers me more than when the news, media, and society tell me I must change to fit their mold. The 2023 Barbie movie had a fantastic monologue that really hit the nail with what society expects of women.

A human who enters Barbie's world is trying to console Barbie, who is in the middle of a minor meltdown after the Kens have taken over her world. Barbie has some feelings of inadequacy, believing she's not good enough for anything.

That's when this average human woman in Barbie's perfect world hits the audience with the pressures of society.

"You have to be thin, but not too thin… You have to have money, but you can't ask for it… You have to be a boss, but you can't be mean… You're supposed to stay pretty but not too pretty to be tempting… Never get old, never be rude, never show off, never be selfish…"

I realize that men also have standards and pressures from the same sources. The above reference is only meant to showcase how society creates these unrealistic expectations.

Self-acceptance isn't changing for someone else. It's not living up to someone else's standards. It's not 'being okay' with something that *you* believe should change. It's not an excuse to stay stuck or to be rude to someone.

Self-acceptance is when you embrace everything about you, not just the positive. It's taking the parts of you that need work and polish and accepting that they are what they are. It's also putting a realistic plan in place to improve the things you want to improve.

There was a time after I took a Landmark Forum class when I would introduce myself, saying, "Hi, I'm Bobbie, and I'm an arrogant asshole." Now, sure, that's an interesting opening and can certainly start a conversation. But it also gave me permission to continue being an arrogant asshole. I just told them I was, so they should expect it from me. So, while this is a way to practice self-acceptance, it also gave me an excuse not to change if I didn't want to.

Instead of immediately working to correct our behavior, self-acceptance has us start by accepting that we do, act, or are the way we are. Once we have that part figured out, we can uncover what's underneath our behavior and actions. In a nutshell, self-acceptance is saying this is where I am, but it may not be where I want to be.

The good news is you are not just negative. There are some amazing and incredible parts present in your life as well. Self-acceptance recognizes those aspects of you, too.

In learning to accept yourself, blemishes and all, you give yourself permission to not be perfect all the time. You are, after all, human, and humans can really mess things up. That doesn't make you broken or not good enough. It makes you authentic.

That statement is powerful enough that it bears repeating. You are not broken, and you don't *need* fixing. You are a beautiful person, inside and out. You, and you alone, determine the person you want to become.

Self-acceptance is not just about accepting what you *are*, though. It's also about accepting what happened to you. When you take stock of your past, make sure you include the trauma and less-than-awesome events that you experienced.

"Acceptance" is not the same thing as saying, "this is okay." You can accept something that happened to you and still not forgive the event or the behavior of someone who hurt you. You are not absolving anything. You are merely accepting that it occurred. No more hiding. You are now facing it head-on.

A Note About Blame and Forgiveness

I want to briefly touch on the notion of blame and forgiveness. No matter what happened to you in the past or what was done to you, blaming yourself is counterproductive. You are responsible for the way you act and the things you do. You are NOT responsible for the way others act and what they do. When you say, "I'm sorry" for something that is not your fault, it is a form of accepting blame. If you blame yourself for something someone else did, it's another scenario to add to your list of things to work on with your inner child.

I could write a whole book on forgiveness. When you're doing inner work, the purpose of forgiveness is for you. You can and should forgive yourself for holding onto situations that don't serve you, for beating yourself up over how you should or shouldn't act, and for allowing someone else to live in your head rent-free. You can choose to forgive someone who hurt you or not. The choice is yours. But you must forgive yourself.

Daily Practices for Self-Acceptance

I'm a big fan of journaling because it's like talking to a friend without having to worry about any potential judgment. You can explore the entirety of your emotions, no matter how negative or ugly they might seem — and there is something so freeing about getting those thoughts on paper.

You can do the following daily practices in a journal, or you can do them in other ways. The point is to make it a habit. James Clear, author of Atomic Habits, says to do your best to be 1% better every day. The compounding effect of being only 1% better every day means by the end of one year, you have improved by 3778%. That's 37 times better than when you started!

1. **Daily Gratitude:** I always start the day with gratitude. At the beginning of the day, write three things you are grateful for. It's ok to start small. I am grateful I have lungs and can breathe. Or I am grateful for the air. Your gratitude doesn't have to be for anything deep in the beginning. Just start the habit. Over time, you may realize how many things you have to be grateful for. I make it a personal challenge to be grateful for different things throughout the week and not be repetitive of the things I'm thankful for in a 7-day stretch. As time passes, you might realize you are grateful for more and more things.
2. **Reframe Your Negative Thoughts:** Your inner voice can be really loud sometimes. However, instead of trying to drown them out, try flipping the script. Take what the voice says to you and give it a more positive spin. If the voice said, "I'm a screwup," flip it to "I am good at finding ways not to do something." Recognize the thought, but reframe it into something with a more compassionate tone. Instead of saying something like, "I'm a mess," when you make a mistake, try something like, "I am human. I do the best I can."
3. **Forgiveness:** A daily practice of forgiveness is another great way to work on self-acceptance. Again, this doesn't need to be big, but what's one thing you can forgive yourself for? It could be a snide remark to a friend, a petty moment with an ex, or thinking negative thoughts about yourself. There are lots of moments in our daily lives that we can and should forgive ourselves for.

I love to start my day on a positive note. It helps me set the tone for the day. So, most of my daily practices are done in the morning. For you, it may feel right to use your daily practice as a wind-down routine. Either way works. Pick a time to do your daily self-acceptance and build the habit. You'll be amazed at how much growth you have with regular moments like this.

When you embrace yourself, warts and all, you take a critical step forward on your journey of healing. Self-acceptance is a path to healing because it is, at its core, acknowledging all parts of yourself. You are showing your inner child that it's okay. You will work on problems together, acknowledge the pain, and show compassion to yourself.

EXERCISE: PERCEPTUAL POSITIONS

Sometimes, we need a little more information to help us through a situation. This exercise is a fantastic way to gather information you might have missed when it happened.

We start out by understanding the three key players ina given memory.

1. **You:** This is the event from your point of view. It's looking at the world through your own eyes. It's what you saw, what you heard, and what you felt in the moment.
2. **The Other Person:** This is only a place to gather information. We do not judge or try to "become" the other person. We simply use this viewpoint to see how *we* come across.
3. **A Viewer:** This is the viewpoint of an observer like someone watching your memory on TV. From this point of view, you are not invested in the outcome or the

event. There are no emotions from this view, and it is a more rational, impartial view.

This exercise gains information about yourself and the event you may not have had before. So, you can determine what—if anything—you can do to be the person you desire to be. It's a way to analyze your behavior retroactively and then choose to improve. It will increase your own self-awareness of how you act in relationships and with others around you.

1. Pick an event that you'd like more clarity on. Start with something simple, like getting upset at another driver on the way to work or losing your cool with your kids. This exercise is best done on something you currently deal with. The more recent the situation, the better. It will help you notice how your inner child is expressing themselves in a less-than-helpful way.
2. Write each player listed above on an index card and lay them on the floor in front of you in the shape of an inverted triangle. The Viewer is closest to you. "You" is to your left and a little further away. The Other Person is to your right, in line with the first position.
3. Step on The Viewer card and play out the scene in front of you with *you* in the "You" position and *the other person* in the other position. Watch the scene unfold in front of you like you're watching a movie.
4. Notice what is going on in the scene. What do you see from here? What do you hear from here? Do you have any new information from watching the interaction from here?
5. Now, step onto the "You" card and face the "Other Person" card. Watch the event unfold from your point of

view. See what you saw, hear what you heard, feel what you felt.
6. What new information do you have now that you've watched the event from this point of view? What did you feel? Name it. What did you see? Did you miss anything? What did you hear? Do you hear anything different than you did before?
7. Step off of the "You" card and back on The Viewer. What information did you pick up? Any insights at this point?
8. Now, step onto the "Other Person" card. Here, all you are doing is SEEING what happened from the other person's point of view. You are not judging or trying to guess what's going on in the other person's world. You are simply gathering data on how *you* show up to the other person.
9. Again, step back onto the viewer card. Notice what new information you now have from checking out the situation from both points of view.
10. Take a moment and write your findings. Was there something you didn't like about how you reacted? Write it down. That can be something to investigate further. Was there something you missed while IN the interaction that might have changed your reaction? Write it down. Maybe you'll catch something similar next time and avoid your undesired response.

The more self-awareness you have, the easier it becomes to recognize patterns in your life and take the steps to adjust as needed.

EXERCISE: SELF-ACCEPTANCE JOURNAL PROMPTS

Here are a few journal prompts that can strengthen your self-acceptance muscles.

- **Today, I choose to accept _____ about me because_____**
- **A piece of advice I would give my younger self is _____**
- **My younger self could really use a _____ right now because_____**
- **I will say "No" more in _____ area of my life because_____**

Journal prompts help to get your feelings out of your body and on paper. It's a way for you to release your emotions and thoughts about certain things instead of keeping them inside. You never have to share your journal with anyone. So go ahead, open up, and set yourself free.

4
THE POWER OF BOUNDARIES

You have to love and respect yourself enough to not let people use and abuse you. You have to set boundaries and keep them. Let people clearly know how you won't tolerate to be treated, and let them know how you expect to be treated.

— JEANNETTE CORON

BOUNDARIES 101

No is one of the most powerful personal statements we can make. It's a complete sentence, and it marks a boundary of something we're not willing to do or tolerate. It's also one of the hardest things for some woman to say[19]. Not because we can't say the word but because, over the years, we've been trained to think that "no" is selfish. "No" is a woman avoiding her duties to other people.

With boundaries, "no" is a start. However, let's define what a boundary is and what it isn't.

Dr. Sharon Martin, psychotherapist and mental health contributor for Physchology Today, states, "A boundary is an imaginary line that separates me from you. It separates your physical space, your feelings, and responsibilities from others.[22]" Boundaries are lines you draw to tell people where you begin. It's a way of telling people how to interact with you. They can be a physical boundary, such as "I don't give hugs;" an emotional boundary, such as "I don't have the capacity to talk about this right now;" or a way you choose to be treated, "I will not be spoken to like that."

One problem in society today is we have lost the art of setting, respecting, and maintaining boundaries for ourselves and those we interact with. Solid, clear boundaries are extremely important for our safety and sanity. You've probably interacted with people that either don't have good boundaries themselves, or maybe they don't respect your boundaries.

An easy-to-understand example of boundaries comes with your home and your property. Whether you own or rent a single-family home or live in an apartment, condo, or something in between, your contract shows defined boundaries of your living space. It may include the lot size, the specific door number to your space, and any other rules, regulations, and amenities you have access to or ownership of. These are usually clearly defined. If you rent, your agreement for renting tells you what you can and can't do with the property, and if you own, you'll get the area clearly defined as yours.

Now, using this example, what would happen if a boundary were crossed? Let's say your neighbor comes into your garden and picks a flower. Has a boundary been crossed? Yes. Unless you've given explicit permission for your neighbor to take a flower, then the physical boundary of your home has been crossed. In this example, you have legal backing to enforce your boundary.

What happens if someone enters your home without your permission? Is this another form of crossing boundaries? Absolutely. Again, you have legal recourse to back up and enforce your boundary.

I should point out that in both examples, the boundaries were clearly set with a document in place to help enforce the boundary. You did not give permission for the person to violate the boundary. Where things get murky and harder to deal with is if you give permission for someone to come and pick up your flowers. Or you give permission to someone to enter your home. In the same situations, the lines of your boundaries become a little fuzzier. This does not give someone the right to cross your boundaries, but it makes the situation a little harder to separate.

The same is true of your personal boundaries. The clearer and more defined you make them, the more consistent you are with setting and enforcing them, and the easier it is for you to enforce. These clear boundaries help you avoid uncomfortable situations later down the road. Boundaries are not "mean," and they are not selfish. They are vital to your physical and mental well-being.

Physical Boundaries

Physical boundaries concern your physical body and health. They can include if and how you allow people to touch you. They may include how much space you need between you and another person. A physical boundary might look like not hugging certain people. It could also look like asking for personal space or even making it clear what you want to occur in the bedroom during intimate moments. Whatever the case, physical boundaries are important because your body is your own.

As children, we are not always given permission to set our own physical boundaries. You may have been told to give certain people hugs. It could be your aunt Mildred, who pinched your cheeks so hard they turned red every time you saw her at Thanksgiving dinner.

For me, I didn't really like being tickled as a child. It always started out as fun, but then the tickling got harder, and the other person's fingers would dig into my side. That hurt, and I didn't like it. It took me several years to be comfortable saying I didn't like to be tickled. I was well into my marriage before I set the boundary of no tickling.

At first, my husband would wonder why I didn't like to be tickled. He'd make fun of me and say it was all fun. However, I kept the hard-line and set a boundary around it. To this day, I don't allow anyone to tickle me. It's not fun for me.

Your physical boundaries are something that might not have been respected when you were a kid. Sometimes, that's because we don't have the right words, and other times, it could be because the adults in your life thought they were doing what's best for you. Now, you get to not only retrain your brain, but you can and should decide how you want your physical body to be touched.

To get started thinking about your physical boundaries, ask yourself the following questions. It's okay to not have a definitive answer just yet. It's also okay for your answers to be situational. The point here is to think about what you want your boundaries to be.

- **Do I feel discomfort somewhere in my body when I am touched without consent?**
- **How can I define my physical boundaries with those who don't respect my space?**
- **Am I comfortable with this person touching me?**
- **Are there certain times or people I have a different level of comfort with?**
- **Where does my physical boundary end?**

Once you know where your physical boundaries are, you can begin to create boundaries around what you want or don't want from other people.

Emotional Boundaries

Emotional boundaries include what you feel comfortable sharing with others. Not everyone needs or deserves your emotional energy. Have you ever been stuck with what I call an energy vampire? These are people who zap your energy because it can be emotionally exhausting to be with them. They often share too much information, or they require you to give and give and give your energy to help them through a problem.

Maybe you're the kind of person who overshares with others. You give a lot of personal details to someone who may or may not have asked for it. Once you've spilled your life's story, you may think, "Why did I just tell them that?"

There are people who show extreme vulnerability when it's not appropriate. An example of this would be crying in your office if you don't get a project you want. It can also be extreme rage if someone tells you something you don't like.

These are all examples of weak emotional boundaries. A weak emotional boundary are either non-existent, or can easily be crossed without consequences. Strong boundaries are ones that you can hold firm even if it gets uncomfortable between you and the other person.

To get started with understanding where your current boundaries are, ask yourself the following questions:

- **What am I comfortable sharing with those close to me?**
- **Who am I comfortable sharing my emotions with?**
- **Are there times I over-share personal information?**
- **Do I have extreme emotions I can't control in certain situations?**
- **Do I "unload" my emotions or problems on someone else?**
- **Do I get sucked into someone else's drama regularly?**

Time Boundaries

We all have 24 hours in a day. We all have seven days a week and 365 days a year. Time is the one thing we can never get back once it's gone. Many gurus, thought leaders, and coaches would tell you it's the only resource you can't make more of. That's why boundaries around our time are critical.

Time boundaries range from your personal use of time, the demand on your time from other people, and how stressed you feel around time.

I hate being late, especially for important events or personal commitments. I will arrange my day around the time I need to spend for an event. I believe my time is important, and I respect other people's time enough not to make them wait for me if we agree on a time. My ex-husband thought of time differently than I did. For him, his time was most important, and he had no problem making others wait for him, even if he was late. Our differing opinions about time boundaries often caused disagreements in our house.

Time boundaries are not just about being on time. They can also include setting a boundary around the time you give to yourself and what you value spending time on.

Dan, a friend of mine, will schedule his life around his surfing time. He prioritizes the waves and uses that time to clear his mind. Another friend, Kelly, prioritizes her family. She will decline meetings and even social gatherings if they occur during her family time.

These are all examples of time boundaries. Here are a few more questions you can use to help you define your time boundaries:

Do I have scheduled time to relax and unwind?

Do I overbook or double-book my time regularly?

When do I spend time on my hobbies?

Do I have a clearly defined start and end time for work and play?

Can I easily say yes or no to other's requests in my time?

When do I go to the gym or prioritize my health?

Do I have a system that works for me to help keep track of my time?

Material Boundaries

At the beginning of this chapter, we discussed boundaries extending beyond your physical, mental, and emotional being. Your boundaries can also extend to your property. This includes your possessions and money. You may set your boundaries on how these things are used, shared, or loaned.

When I was dating, I didn't let my date enter my home until I was ready to introduce them to my life more. I don't loan tools to friends and family because I'm not sure when or if I will ever see them again. I also have a very clear boundary on who gets to use my Nintendo Switch. If my kids are reading this, no, you can't play the game until I beat it first.

One example of a material boundary that can become muddy quickly is money. This includes loaning money to family and friends, creating and adhering to a budget, or even what you buy and when. Money can be a taboo topic for many families because of how we've been raised and what our native culture teaches us about money[8].

With money, bartering can also be a source of pain for several people. What you have has value. What another person has also has value. If you both believe you are making a fair trade, then bartering works. Problems arise when one person feels they got a poor deal. If you've ever felt this way, then you may need to set clear boundaries around your material possessions.

Here are a few questions to get you started thinking about your boundaries for your material items.

- Am I okay with letting someone use my stuff?
- Are there certain people I don't want to share with?
- Do I feel pressured by someone to share my things?

- Have I felt uncomfortable sharing my things in the past?
- Do I feel like saying 'no' would ruin one of my relationships?

The Bottom Line on Boundaries

While this isn't an exhaustive list of boundaries, it's a great place to get started. Before you set a bunch of new boundaries with the people in your life, you want to understand your current boundaries. Do you have boundaries? Do you need to figure out where they are? Where would you like your boundaries to be?

The clearer a picture you can create for yourself, the easier it is to establish and maintain your boundaries with others. Write some goals of where your boundaries currently exist and where you would like them to be. Now you have a roadmap. Let's work on what to do from this point.

FUZZY OR NON-EXISTENT BOUNDARIES

You may already have some firm boundaries, or you may have fuzzy and non-existent boundaries. Now that we've identified where your boundaries are, let's discuss what it may look like when you're not clear on your own boundaries.

Dawn loved her husband most days, but when he came home drinking, she didn't know which version of him she would get. It could be the one who yelled a bit and passed out on the couch or the one who backed her into the corner and threatened to beat her within an inch of her life. She tried to talk to him about his drinking, but he swore he could control it. He often did for a little while, but then something would happen at work, and he'd hit the bars on the way home and start the cycle all over again.

Dawn kept telling me her husband was trying, and he had not put a hand on her *yet*. All he did was threaten and scare her, so it wasn't a big deal. If that's what she had to put up with in her marriage, she could handle it. As long as he didn't bring alcohol into the house, she could overlook his occasional trips to the bar, even though she knew he hid beer in a fridge in the basement.

What you don't know about Dawn is that her father was also an alcoholic. Her father would come home every day and leave a trail of destruction in his wake. He hit her mother, broke furniture, and would scream at Dawn if she was in his line of sight. He praised her brothers for doing 'manly things' and degraded Dawn if she wore a dress out of the house because it showed too much skin and tempted the boys.

Dawn was stuck in a cycle of fuzzy and non-existent boundaries. Because she grew up with few healthy boundaries at home, she continued with the fuzzy boundaries as an adult. She said she would date no one who drank. However, the first time her husband came home drunk, and she did nothing about it, it was the beginning of loose and fuzzy boundaries. When he yelled at her the first time, her boundaries became more blurred. Eventually, she was in a relationship that closely resembled her parents'.

Dawn isn't the only one with boundary issues like this. We've all let a boundary slip from time to time. It's why we find ourselves in jobs we hate, relationships that aren't good for us, or stuck in life. Somewhere along the way, we let our boundaries blur, if we even set them at all.

If you have fuzzy or non-existent boundaries, you may notice that someone you deal with regularly starts taking more and more liberties with you. It rarely starts as a blatant crossing of a boundary. It starts slowly, like a kid testing the rules. They'll push the limits of a boundary, and if nothing is done, they push a little more until they're so far past the boundary that you don't know what happened.

This can happen with big boundaries, like your personal space and touch, and even with little boundaries, like your time or your attention to a specific friend. I had a high school friend that was great if we talked every day. If I didn't call her one day, she would get so mad at me that we couldn't hang out until I apologized for ignoring her. It was emotionally exhausting to deal with her. I thought I could deal with that type of personality until I really needed a friend when my boyfriend broke up with me, and my friend was nowhere to be found. She was only willing to let me deal with her drama but wanted nothing to do with mine.

As an adult, I don't have friends like that anymore. It took me years to discover that was a boundary for me and decide where I wanted to draw the line. Saying no to someone or something shouldn't send you spiraling into fear and shame. Setting boundaries will help you grow as a person and, ultimately, as a friend.

THE COST OF NOT SETTING BOUNDARIES

Boundaries exist to protect you. They help you establish what you will and will not accept. It's exhausting to deal with people who consistently violate your boundaries, and you can even lose yourself along the way if you're not careful.

My ex-husband came home one day and said his business, *our business*, wasn't doing so well. We had an internet marketing company that sold products online and the delay between buying and paying for product and staff, and when sales came in was slow. We needed an influx of cash to keep it going, and he had an idea. He knew that we both had great credit and could get personal loans to support the business. The cash would help get the business out of the hole it was in, and we could pay off the balance in installments. The process was quick, and we could access significantly better interest rates than if we explored a bank loan.

He needed my help, and the employees of the business were counting on us to address this situation. On the surface, it made sense. Small businesses are often funded by personal loans to get them through a difficult time.

That's where sense stopped. Being a dutiful wife, I didn't think twice about it, and I didn't question him. My role as his wife was to support his dream. So, I did what he asked. I applied for as many personal credit cards as I could in a 24-hour period. I was approved for $235,000 in personal credit, and I handed it all over to him. He immediately maxed out every single one of the cards.

The business paid at least the minimum payment every month and then reused the available credit to continue operations. Business was good because of the use of our credit, and life was wonderful—until it wasn't. My ex ran into more and more problems with sales and cashflow, and eventually, the monster he'd created couldn't be maintained. He stopped paying our personal credit cards because, and I quote, "We should be the last ones we take care of for debt."

The minimum monthly payments on my personal credit cards were more than I personally earned in a month. There was no way I could maintain that level of debt. His solution to this was for us to declare bankruptcy together and then rebuild. It's obvious to me now, but I didn't have very good boundaries when it came to money back then.

Money wasn't the only thing my lack of boundaries cost me. My trust was abused and broken, and what little boundaries I did have were severely violated the moment business started failing. Instead of filing for bankruptcy, we ended up getting divorced, and he was all too willing for me to take my debt with me because it was "personal" debt.

Long story short, I discovered how weak my boundaries were when it came to money. I ended up with a long road to recovery from a devastating financial situation and learned a few lessons on what I would and wouldn't allow in the future.

When you allow yourself to bow to someone's demands and violate your boundaries, or what would be a boundary if you had one, there is a power imbalance. Aside from resentment, this can open the door for manipulation and even abuse.

DOES YOUR INNER CHILD AFFECT YOUR BOUNDARIES?

The short answer is yes. I've already given several examples of how something that happens to us when we're a child has long-lasting effects. We learn everything by watching as we grow up. If your family had weak boundaries, you may have weak boundaries as an adult. If your childhood friends had weak boundaries, you may have weak boundaries as an adult. If you didn't have an example of strong, healthy boundaries in your childhood, you must do the work to establish and maintain boundaries as an adult.

Take the boundary of money, for example. If your parents always lived within their means, had a budget, talked about finances with the family, and shared that knowledge with you as a child, you likely have a good foundation for your adult life. However, this taboo topic often gets pushed under the table and spoken about in hushed tones with many families.

When I was growing up, I knew little about my parents' financial situation. I knew when they bought their house in Maryland that it was a stretch for my dad's income, but it wasn't something we couldn't handle with a little sacrifice. I knew my dad kept track of a budget because I would hear things like, "That's not in the budget for this month" or "I need to move money around for that." I even knew my parents had "spending money" where they could buy whatever they wanted each month. My mother would spend much of her time on things for the house. My dad would save him and buy something bigger every few months.

School taught me how to balance a checkbook, but never what happened if you maxed out a credit card. I never knew what would happen if I maxed out a credit card. Nobody taught me the value of investing, and I only had a vague idea of how to save for what I wanted. I didn't understand money or how it worked, which meant I didn't have strong boundaries about what I would and wouldn't allow when it came to my finances.

This was my money foundation. Which created some very fuzzy boundaries as I stepped out into the world of being an adult. Fuzzy boundaries like, "Never spend more than you make, unless you can afford the credit card payment". This is fuzzy for a few reasons. It's not clearly defined and there are ways I can disrespect my own boundary and still somehow justify what I want to buy is within my boundary.

So, when I got out of high school, I learned from the school of hard knocks. As a single woman, I had two car payments, rent for an apartment, and just enough money left over each month to buy basic food. I had no furniture in my apartment except for the bed my parents gave me when I moved out. The back seat of my car was my sofa. I had a small TV sitting on some boxes, pots and pans in the kitchen, and a small Christmas tree (because that was important to me in the first place). I went out and bought a dog. I knew just enough not to completely drown in debt, but I didn't understand what happens if you spend more than you make.

Now you may be saying to yourself that this all sounds like I didn't understand money instead of being a boundary issue. And on the surface you might be right. But think about it like this, I didn't understand that you can't spend more than you make. So I had a very loose personal boundary when I wanted to purchase something. As long as I had money on my credit card I would buy it. Even if that meant I would struggle to make the payments later. I knew enough to make a budget, but didn't understand how to stick to one. Again, I had a loose personal boundary about what I wanted to spend my money on. I would move money around in my budget to afford certain things, or pay for things I'd already bought, and not stick to the boundary I created in my budget and planning.

These lessons from growing up were internalized. I had very weak boundaries around money, and it showed up in different ways. That's what set the foundation for not fully understanding the impact of my ex-husband's request to use my personal credit.

This is just one way my inner child had a tremendous impact on my boundaries. Your inner child impacts you as well. There are four distinct ways you might see boundary issues from your childhood show up.

1. **Fight:** You push your needs onto others and impose your view of events. You might even attack others if you don't feel your needs are met right away. You don't have good boundaries yourself, and you may not respect the boundaries of others. This often looks like asking for

things that may be inappropriate in your need to satisfy your desires.
2. **Flight:** You actively run from problems or issues as they arise. It might look like relationship hopping, changing jobs frequently, or even moving around to avoid issues.
3. **Freeze:** This is a different type of avoidance. You may just ignore the issue until it becomes too big to deal with. You might allow bills to pile up, stay in an unhealthy relationship, or stick with a job because you don't know what to do to get out.
4. **Feign/Submit:** You allow others to control and dictate what you should do. This is another form of avoidance and gives you the ability to either be a victim or pass the blame on someone or something else. You often put everyone else's needs above yours.

When you look at these different responses, you may fall into several of them, and you may have different forms for different situations.

I was stuck in all four of the above issues with money. In my social life, I was in fight-and-freeze mode. With my relationships, I was stuck in a cycle of flight and submission. These boundary issues happen because you may not have a great example of setting healthy boundaries, so you have found different ways to address them in your adult life.

HOW TO SET HEALTHY BOUNDARIES

Your inner child and you need a solid way to set boundaries for yourself. You also need to recognize when your boundaries are being tested, or not respected and how you should handle those situations. Plus, you need to respect other people's boundaries as well. Your journey of healing can't happen if you violate the boundaries of the people in your life or continue to allow others to violate your boundaries.

My oldest son isn't a big hugger. He's been that way most of his life. I am a HUGE hugger. So, sometimes, our physical touch was mismatched. After working on myself a lot, I realized I may have been forcing my son to do something he's not comfortable with. Now, I ask him if I can have a hug, and I respect his response. Sometimes he's open to it, sometimes he gives me a 'side hug,' and sometimes he says no. He sets his boundaries, and I respect and honor them. It's a beautiful way for me to teach and show him not only how to set boundaries, but how to respect another person's boundaries as well.

Identify or Create Your Boundaries

Where are you struggling? Where do you feel drained and frustrated? Where do you feel taken advantage of? This is a good place to start and might be a sign of a lack of boundaries.

Look at what you are no longer willing to do or put up with and ask yourself why. Create a list of what you are unwilling to compromise on. When you have a clear picture of what you *don't* want, try making a list of what you *do* want to experience, such as joy or respect. This gives you a better understanding of where those gaps are in your boundaries.

I didn't like it when I was late for things. I really didn't like it when my ex was the reason I was late. I would constantly give the 'leave time' for when I wanted to leave, and he would habitually start getting ready five minutes before that time. Without fail, he needed 'five more minutes' when I wanted to leave. If we left the house late, I would stress over being late or missing whatever it was I wanted to do completely. We were often late to things because I waited for him and we got stuck in traffic, or he took so long to get ready that we missed the first 30 minutes to an hour of an event.

So, I tried to create a boundary around my leave time. I put time and effort into calculating backward from the time I wanted to arrive, how long it would take to get there, when I wanted to leave, and when I had to get ready. This was the first step in creating my boundary. I made a statement to myself about what my boundary was. "I will leave at this time."

Another example of a boundary I set was when my ex would drink directly from the milk carton in the fridge and then put it back. He didn't grab a cup because he only wanted a sip. We had a family of four who all drank milk, and, for me, this was disgusting and disrespectful. I created a boundary around the milk. I made a statement to myself. "This is community milk, not a personal glass." We'll talk more about these situations in a moment because this is only the beginning of setting a boundary.

Setting boundaries is an act of love toward yourself and others. You want to protect your peace of mind, and you want to be open and honest about them with those around you. Boundaries are firm but flexible. Sometimes, your boundaries need to change because you don't need them anymore or because you have changed and need to update them. So, don't feel you must be perfect or permanent with creating and identifying your boundaries.

Here are a few tips as you set boundaries.

- **Understand Your Priorities.** Start with a few small boundaries as you go through the process. Once you've established a boundary or two and feel better about setting it, then you should focus on the boundaries that can change your life. The things you focus on become the things that change and grow. So, set your priorities on which boundaries you want to tackle first and take them on one at a time.

- **Get Comfortable Being Uncomfortable.** When you draw lines for how you want to be treated, you might feel uncomfortable. You may feel guilt, uneasiness, or even awkwardness if you aren't used to setting a line and holding it. This is normal. Maintaining boundaries is a skill. At first, you may be a little shaky when using your new skill, but over time, it gets easier and easier.
- **Allow Space for Your Feelings.** It's important to have a plan for what happens when someone crosses your boundaries. It is almost more important than the boundary itself. However, setting boundaries, and dealing with someone crossing them can trigger some emotions. Give yourself the grace and space you need to deal with your emotions. It's okay if you don't address a boundary right away if you need time to process what you're feeling. Don't take too long, though; the sooner you can address a boundary, the more likely you will feel relief.
- **Respect the Boundaries of Others.** Respect is a two-way street. As you go about setting boundaries for yourself, respect the boundaries of others. It's okay if you have different boundaries from the people in your life. You can and should still respect their boundary. If you have competing boundaries, respect the most restrictive of the boundaries. For example, you may be a hugger who is willing to hug when you first meet. You may run across someone who doesn't like to be hugged and certainly not when they first meet. This person has a

more restrictive boundary than you do and you should respect their boundaries about touch.

A Statement, an Order, or a Boundary—Which is it?

No matter how much we may *think* we can or how hard we try, we cannot control other people. You can only take responsibility for yourself and your actions. Therefore, it's extremely important we take a moment and talk about how you communicate your boundaries with everyone around you. There are three ways to communicate, but only one is a true boundary.

For example, a statement is something like, "I don't like when you treat me this way" or "That doesn't make me feel good." These statements make a declaration, but they are not boundaries.

Likewise, an order is a demand you place on someone else. "You will treat me with respect." This is a rule that someone else must follow. It's trying to control someone else's actions and behavior.

A boundary is when you tell the other person where the line for you is and then what you will do about it if it gets crossed. "If you don't treat me with respect, I will walk away from this conversation." This shows the other person how you will respond when they cross a line you've set for yourself.

The clearer you are when you communicate to people what you will and won't tolerate, the easier it is for them to make a choice, and yes, they have a choice. They can choose to accept your boundaries or not. The difference is what you will do.

Remember the two boundaries I set earlier with my ex? The first one of *I will leave at this time* was really an order instead of a boundary. And I eventually changed it to, "This is what time I want to leave, if you are not ready, I will leave without you." The second boundary of community milk and not a personal glass was also an order instead of a boundary. It was updated to, "This is community milk, if you continue to use it as a personal glass I will no longer buy milk by the gallon and we will all have single serving milks."

Now, it's easier to get people to listen to you if you start the conversation about boundaries in the right way. This is a change in how you want and expect to be treated, so it's best to stay calm and kind when you address the other person. Not everyone is trying to hurt you intentionally, so give the other person the benefit of the doubt when you first talk to them about your boundary.

Make sure you are clear and specific. Don't dance around the issue! Get right to the heart of the matter. It should be focused on what you want, what you don't want, and, if appropriate, one or two times where the boundary may have been crossed in the past. For most people, this should be enough for them to decide to respect your boundaries.

The Discomfort of Setting Boundaries

When you first set a boundary, it can be an uncomfortable experience. You are telling people who are close to you and people you interact with regularly that they have hurt you. That's an uncomfortable conversation, no matter how you slice it. But the value for yourself and your relationship with the other person far outweighs the moment of discomfort.

When my firstborn was six months old, I decided to go back to college and finish my degree. Both my husband and I worked, so trying to juggle everything with a baby was incredibly difficult. I asked my mom if she would help with her grandson two weekends a month so I could spend that time studying.

Things started off very well. We would meet halfway between homes, hug as we moved the car seat and kid between cars, and go on about with life. Sometimes, we swapped stories or experiences of interacting with my baby. As the weeks rolled on, my mother would get a little more accusatory in her suggestions about what I should or shouldn't be doing. When the comments first started, I would brush them off as advice that I didn't have to address. However, the comments kept coming. "Why would you let him cry like that?" "You're ruining this kid." "If you keep up like this, your kid won't love anybody or know how to love."

I was certain my mother and I just needed to figure out how our relationship was changing from mother-daughter to grandma-mom-son. If my mom could take a step back and just be a grandma and allow me to make my own mistakes or discover my way to be a mom, then we'd be fine. After all, I really needed her help as I was going through school and working.

One day, on a call with my mom about the upcoming weekend exchange, I snapped. I didn't want to be told I was a terrible mom anymore, and I didn't know what to do about the constant comments. So, I told her, in a not-so-pleasant and calm tone, that if she continued to feel the need to tell me how bad a parent I was, then I no longer needed her help, and my son would stay away from her.

It was one of the hardest things I've ever had to do, but I couldn't continue the way things were. I didn't want to cut my mom out of my life, but I also didn't want to be berated because I chose to raise my kid differently than she would have.

We talked about it over the phone. My dad got on the line as well. We decided that complete separation was not what either of us wanted. She would hold back her harsh criticism, and when I wanted advice, I would ask about something specific. We created a boundary for both of us to keep our relationship healthy.

Sometimes, you need to be firm and decisive. Let the other person know what's a "no-go" for you. When they have a clear picture of your deal breakers and the consequences of how you will act if they cross your line, they get to make their own choice.

Don't be afraid of resolution! There are plenty of situations where you might find that violations occur through no malice of the other person. If this is a new boundary, sometimes people slip. It's important that you do not shy away from having a healthy conversation about what occurred and how it made you feel.

This incident was nearly 14 years ago. And it took us a while to navigate the new boundaries we had in place. And thankfully we were both willing to put in the work. Because 14 years later my mom and I have an amazing relationship, and my son is just fine. I still ask her for advice, and she still tells me what she thinks, but it no longer feels like a personal attack on me. It took a very hard conversation for us to even have a chance at a normal relationship, and I am forever grateful for it. I love my mom, and I'm glad she's in my life. It wasn't an overnight change for us, and it most likely won't be for you, either. The key is to stay consistent with how you manage, communicate, and ultimately handle the boundaries you set.

Repeated Boundary Crossers

There are some people in this world who choose to ignore the boundaries of others. Perhaps they struggle with their own boundary issues, or perhaps they don't respect the line you have drawn. Whatever the case may be, it's important to address when they cross your boundaries every time. Your boundaries deserve to be respected. If someone repeatedly ignores or disrespects your boundaries and you've had conversations with them about what's going on, it's up to you to decide when enough is enough. It's okay to cut someone out of your life if they choose to violate your boundaries.

EXERCISE: THE FIRST TIME

It's challenging to uncover boundary issues you may have. A simple exercise you can do to help you find the first time a specific boundary showed up in your life is by using a timeline.

1. Start by thinking of an issue or problem you're having with someone right now. It doesn't have to be the worst thing you're dealing with. It can be an argument with a coworker or struggling with time management.
2. Imagine your timeline on the floor in front of you. Your past is laid out to your left, the present directly in front of you, and your future is laid out to the right.
3. Step on your timeline in the "present" and face your future.
4. Take a moment and describe the issue you're working on.
5. Slowly step backward into your past as you collect times that are like the issue at hand. *NOTE: If you have a*

troublesome event in your past that you don't want to deal with or isn't related to your current issue, just step over it.
6. Continue to move back into the past until you have reached the earliest memory relevant to the problem you're facing.
7. Note how old you are at this moment and give the space you are currently in a name.
8. Step *off* the timeline. Now, as the adult you are with all your experiences and knowledge, determine what resources you needed as a child at the moment that would help you overcome this earliest memory.
9. Once you know what you need, recall a time in your life when you had that resource (even if it was only for a few minutes) and bring that resource with you as you step back onto your timeline in the same space you had your earliest memory.
10. Walk forward along your timeline with your new resource into each space along the path that you collected, and don't forget to step over any issues you didn't want to deal with until you have reached the present day.
11. How has your current issue changed? Notice what's different.
12. Now, it's time to imagine yourself going forward into the future. Step six months into the future when you might experience the issue again and notice how it feels different.
13. Examine how it makes you feel. Now, step back off the timeline.

The resource you identified and brought with you is now fully available to you and your inner child as you experience similar situations now and in the future.

THE BOTTOM LINE

Clear boundaries ensure you are comfortable and safe within your own life. While it is imperative to set them, it's equally important for you to communicate them to others and follow through with what you say will happen if your boundaries are crossed.

FREE GOODWILL

People who help others expecting nothing in return experience a greater sense of fulfillment and have a better life. I'd like to create the opportunity to deliver this value to you during your reading or listening experience. In order to do so, I have a simple question for you.

Would you help someone you've never met if it didn't cost you money, but you never got credit for it?

If so, I have an 'ask' to make on behalf of someone you do not know. And likely, never will. They are just like you, or like you were a few years ago: wanting to know more about their inner child, full of desire to help the world, seeking information but unsure where to look… this is where you come in.

The only way for us at Vital Skills Publishing to accomplish our mission of helping people become the best version of themselves is first, by reaching them. And most people do, in fact, judge a book by its cover (and its reviews). If you have found this book valuable this far, would you please take a brief moment right now and leave an honest review of the book and its contents? It will cost you zero dollars and less than 60 seconds.

Your review helps:

- one more person connect with their inner child
- one more soul begin the process of becoming who they were meant to be
- one more life change for the better

To make that happen... takes less than 60 seconds... and is super simple to do... please leave a review.

<u>If you are on Audible -</u> hit the three dots in the top right of your device, click rate & review, then leave a few sentences about the book with a star rating.

<u>If you are reading on kindle or an e-reader</u> - you can scroll to the bottom of the book, then swipe up, and it will automatically prompt a review.

<u>If you are reading this book as a paper or hardback</u> - you can go to the place where you purchased the book and leave a review there.

If the review process has changed since the publishing of this book, please leave a review on the Amazon book page.

PS—Life hack: If you introduce something valuable to someone, they associate that value with you. If you'd like goodwill directly from another person, send this book their way.

Thank you from the bottom of my heart.

- Bobbie

5
REPARENT YOURSELF

Your inner child still needs to be loved in order to heal the complete self.

— KAREN A. BAQUIRAN

We can't go back in time and change the past, but we can use the resources and experiences we've gained over time and help our inner child grow past the thing that keeps them stuck. This is called reparenting. It's when you, as an adult, work with your inner child the way you wanted or needed someone to do for you as a child. Reparenting is the ultimate in self-care. It's giving yourself what you need.

Your parents might have been unwilling or unable to give you the exact emotion or support you needed growing up. This doesn't mean they were intentionally cruel or hurtful. We are all human and do the best we can in this crazy and sometimes overwhelming world. Sometimes, things slip through the cracks. This is not an excuse or trying to minimize what happened to you as a child. This doesn't erase the hurt someone caused you. However, by showing up for yourself now, you show you are worth the time and effort to be cared for.

You may have a lot of experience as a parent yourself, or you may have very little experience with raising children. Either way, you have already begun healing the wounds of your past. That's the foundation of reparenting. And while we're in this process, let's talk about four guiding pillars to help you along the way.

1. **Discipline:** For some of us, the word discipline has a terrible or even terrifying connotation. It may have been a belt, a switch, a paddle, or something worse in your home growing up. It may have been yelling and screaming or being told to stand in a corner and ignored. Or it may have been a stern talking to and helpful ways to do it better. Discipline is essential for growth and there is a way to show discipline without abusing it. And in the context of reparenting the proper use of discipline is what's needed to create habits and rituals that have a positive influence on your life.
2. **Self-Care:** Don't let the influencers fool you! Self-care isn't all about expensive coffee and retail therapy. Rather, self-care is actively looking out for yourself as you navigate through life. This can be something as simple as making sure you eat three meals a day, drink enough water, or even shower regularly. It could be a special trip to the spa, a float tank, or scheduled alone and "down time." Self-care is taking care of yourself and your needs.
3. **Joy/Wonder:** As a child, we often looked at the world with joy and wonder. We played every chance we got, and we had pirate battles with nothing more than a stick, a blade of grass, and a paper towel roll. We were

dreamers, creative and inquisitive, and the entire world was available to us. Reconnecting to this part of childhood is one of the best ways to begin the healing process. It's not about reconnecting to any pain or lack we had as a child. It's reconnecting to the child-like ability to create our own reality. This may start as a simple skip the next time you walk somewhere or take a detour through a wooded path to see what you find. Or maybe even sitting down with your favorite drink, opening up a journal, and letting your pen do the dreaming for you.

4. **Emotional Regulation:** A large part of the reparenting process is learning how to co-regulate with your inner child. This means you and your inner child work together on emotional control. It's noticing when you need time and space to process your emotions and keeping them in check when you need to. This can be something like breathwork, challenging negative thoughts, or counting down from ten. You and your inner child need to be on the same page to avoid an emotional explosion out of nowhere.

Children learn from their parents, teachers, and friends. They learn by modeling and mimicking behaviors. We're wired to pick up cues from the people we spend the most time with. That's why you'll often see children imitating their parents when they play house or a child acting like the boss of a company if one of their parents brings their work home.

My friend Lindsay had a potty mouth. Spending a few years in the Navy didn't help her language. She embodied the ability to cuss like a sailor. One day, she was taking her 3-year-old daughter to daycare when, from the back seat, she heard her daughter ask,

"Mom, what's f*cking kiddin' me?" Lindsay realized at that moment the words that had just come out of her mouth after someone cut her off on the highway. Her daughter was the perfect parrot of everything mommy was doing.

Everytime I remember this story it makes me laugh, but it also helps to illustrate my point. As children we learned and discovered from those around us. And the same happens when you reparent yourself. Your inner child can learn from the adult you. So it's time to show the child within some of the skills you may or may not have had modeled for you growing up.

Self-Talk

What we say to and about ourselves creates our reality. If we were told as kids that we're bad at math, we may continue to believe that our whole lives. We start said that we can't calculate the tip without our phones or a calculator because "we're bad at math." Maybe you always heard your parents say you are a screw-up. If you take that on and tell yourself the reason your life is a mess is that you're a screw-up, you might look for ways to mess up your life. Self-talk is not just what we say out loud. It's what we think in our minds. Our thoughts become our reality.

The process of healing begins with your thoughts. Journaling and affirmations can help create a new way of thinking. This means a change in self-talk and the beginning of a new life.

Self-Confidence

Confidence can only be learned through experience[42]. When we have success in something, even if it's small, we develop confidence. If we can recreate that success again, our confidence grows. Failure is a part of growth. We must understand that failure isn't the end. It's feedback. It's showing you that the specific way you tried something didn't work. That doesn't mean that every way you try something won't work; rather, it means that very specific way you tried. If we let failure stop us from doing something again, our confidence weakens, and we may give up on a dream before it even takes flight.

When I was eight, my parents enrolled me in violin lessons. At first, I made a lot of mistakes. I couldn't keep the bow from touching more than one string at a time. My fingers didn't go to the right spots to make beautiful sounds. For the first few months of learning to play, I was not good. I remember my teacher telling me I'd never be good at music because I couldn't even get the simplest concepts down. So, naturally, I threw the violin at the teacher and swore off ever playing music again.

If it hadn't been for my father, I may never have picked up another instrument in my life. He said the violin may not have been the best instrument for me. I loved the sound of the flute, and my school offered lessons. My dad looked at me and said, let's give this another shot. Thankfully, I did. Music continues to be a big part of my life, and I play a wide range of instruments (*except the violin!*).

Excellent Communication Skills

Communication isn't just about proper sentence structure and grammar. The real art of communication is about transferring an idea or thought between two or more people so everyone understands the same idea. Unfortunately, this rarely happens between two people. I can't tell you how many times in my life I thought I was having one type of conversation with someone, only to find out they thought we were talking about something completely different. Or when I said something and it was taken the wrong way by the person I was talking to. Communication is bigger than your words and how you use them. It's your thoughts, your words, your body language, and the energy you use.

Let's take the simple question, "How are you?" At face value, this seems like an easy idea to communicate. If you're talking to a favorite aunt who you haven't seen in a few months, you may have a lot of excitement about this question. If you're talking to a coworker who is always late with their reports and causes you stress, the question may come out condescending or ungenuine.

Research on the topic of communication is split on what percentage of communication is verbal and what is non-verbal[14]. This includes tone when speaking, facial expressions, and even your thoughts. Yes, your thoughts can have a tremendous impact on your communication skills. Have you ever thought, "I can't stand this person," right before you've had to speak with them? I'll bet that conversation didn't go very well.

Our goal in reparenting is to give our younger self the skills we needed or missed when growing up. This is why so many of the exercises in this book talk about bringing the resources you have now as an adult back to your memory as a child. It's the best way for your inner child to heal from their hurt and help you as an adult to move forward in a more productive way.

WHAT YOUR INNER CHILD NEEDS FROM YOU

Your inner child wants to feel loved. They want to know someone is looking out for them and keeping them safe. They want to know they can learn and grow and experience the world on their own terms. Isn't that what most children want? However, that message may have been lost over the years through experiences of being shut down, unheard, or ignored.

Maybe, as a child, you believed that love had to be earned through good grades, accomplishments, and good behavior. Your parents might have failed to let you know you are inherently lovable. This can damage how your inner child feels about themselves and how you may feel about yourself as an adult.

Maybe as a child, you believed you were not worth someone else's time; a quick moment to look at a picture you drew, throwing the ball out back with your parents, or even all having dinner together at the table talking about your day. If we don't get these moments growing up, we often keep the belief that we are not worth it.

When you take the time to reparent yourself, you want to rewrite that story. Allow yourself to feel valuable. reminded yourself of this often with powerful affirmations like *"I am loved"* and *"I am worth it."* Look yourself in the eyes when you're standing in front of your mirror and say your affirmations to yourself. For a list of affirmations designed to help heal your inner child, visit www.vitalskillspress.com/innerchild-resources.

No matter what you experienced growing up, your inner child needs you to show them you made it through. They need you to show them the love, the emotions, and the support you wanted in childhood. You have everything you need right now to help heal the missing pieces from your childhood. It may be necessary to start with *"I'm sorry"* or *"It wasn't your fault,"* but it's critical for you to start.

If you're having trouble going to what may be a dark place, it's okay. Some experiences are best worked through with a qualified professional. Don't go to a place you might have a hard time coming out of.

It is also important to acknowledge everything your inner child did *right*. They got you through 100% of your bad days. They were there for it all, and their resilience deserves to be recognized. Take a moment to thank your inner child for all they have done for you. Truly mean it.

Despite the highs and lows, you need to realize that you did the best you could in every situation you've ever been in. As a child, you only had so much knowledge, experience, and capability to deal with life. That's part of the journey we're all on.

THE JOURNEY OF REPARENTING

There is no *one* path to reparenting. Everyone's journey is unique. Here are a few key tips to remember as you navigate working with your inner child.

- **Be Compassionate.** You didn't choose to have these wounds. So, be kind and gentle with yourself. A little compassion for what you experienced and how far you've come goes a long way.
- **Honor Your Feelings.** Your feelings and emotions are always there. They are real; they are valid. You may have been taught that some emotions are "good" while others are "bad," but what you're feeling is neither good nor bad. It just is. Emotions and feelings will always happen. Our goal is to respond to them healthily.
- **Embrace Your Curiosity.** Be open to whatever happens while you address the wounds of your past. Be curious about what may really go on and what you may have needed at the moment. Explore and dream about what you want life to be for you. Create your reality from your curiosity.
- **Remain Consistent.** Healing takes time and, most importantly, consistent treatment. The coping mechanisms we created over the years that have helped

to keep us alive are deeply rooted in who we are. It will take consistent work and consistent healing to forge new habits.
- **Seek Joy!** Reparenting is not just about hard work. Sometimes, the best form of healing is to let go and have fun. Seek things that make you truly happy.
- **Focus on Self-Care.** This process is all about you. It's about becoming the person you are. In order to do this, you need to focus on caring for yourself. This can look like all kinds of things, from eating healthy and setting boundaries to going to therapy and cutting off toxic relationships.
- **Keep Your Promises.** They are the foundation of the changes we want to make. It can start with something as simple as "I will walk for five minutes every day." As long as we keep this promise to ourselves, we are building on a foundation of strength. We prove to ourselves that we can keep our word and we are someone who can be trusted. Start by making small promises and build that over time.
- **CELEBRATE.** This work is a process, and it takes courage. You deserve to celebrate your achievements. Big or small, any movement you make in the process of healing is worth celebrating.

LIVING UP TO THE EXPECTATIONS OF OTHERS

There is a lot of pressure to grow up. We had so many things we needed to learn, from how to read and write to what clothes to wear to school and which ones we could play outside in, and so many other things in between. Children are often overwhelmed by meeting the expectations set for them.

That's why you need to be understanding of any additional pressure you might place on your inner child. Acknowledge their struggle and give them strategies to handle all the expectations.

After getting over my initial distaste for the violin, music came easy to me. I won't say I was a savant or anything like that, but I could play a lot of different instruments with very little effort. This set the bar of expectations high for me. My father was very proud of all the instruments I could "just pick up and play" and would tell everyone about it. Sometimes, I felt he over-exaggerated what I was capable of, and I would choke a little inside with the expectation he had set. I don't believe he did it to see me fail. I believe he was proud of me, but this pride came at a cost.

I felt more and more pressure to perform every time he mentioned how good I was. I would shy away from playing for any reason. When the family was around, there was always a mention of getting the guitar out to play for everyone. I would hem and haw and come up with any excuse I could think of to avoid the pressure. I even made up an excuse that my fingernails were too long, and I didn't have fingernail clippers, so I couldn't play the guitar. All because I didn't want to fail in trying to live up to his expectations.

Even as an adult, I've struggled with putting myself out there for fear of being exposed or not meeting someone else's expectations. Writing this book wasn't difficult until this section. It's hard to put these words on a page. My body is fighting me the entire way by making my fingers heavy, developing pressure in my temple. My inner child is showing up in new and different ways to protect me from the expectations others may have of me.

The expectations of others have an enormous impact on you. Be kind to yourself and give yourself all the compassion you need. If you feel overwhelmed or like you're not meeting the unspoken expectations of where you "should" be on your journey, take a step away from work, have a glass of water, and regroup. It's okay to work at your own pace.

EXERCISE: A LETTER TO YOUR INNER CHILD

You have made it through 100% of the days you've had. The good, the bad, the ugly, and everything in between. Take a moment and write a letter to your younger self. What advice would you give? What did you need or want to know back then but was never told? If you could go back in time to encourage, love, hug, or hold your younger self, what would you do or say?

You may need to address any skepticism you have about someone from the future coming back to you, so think of something you could tell your younger self that would make you know it's you. Think about everything you'd need to include in a letter like this. Remember, your inner child's name is the same as yours. Don't address them as "Dear inner child." Allow them to have their name and address them with it.

Once you know how you might start, grab a pen and paper, head to your physical space, and allow yourself to write. Don't overthink it; let the information and the words flow from you. Take as time and space as you need to write your letter.

When you're done, sign your letter. You have the option of re-reading this letter to yourself or just allowing your letter to go unread. The choice is yours. Take a moment and reflect on this experience and acknowledge anything that may have come up for you.

EXERCISE: A LETTER FROM YOUR INNER CHILD

We've talked about giving your inner child a voice, and now it's time to hear what they have to say. A letter is a great way to share feelings that may be inexpressible. If you think back to when you were a child, it may have been hard for you to talk to an adult about what you were struggling with. Writing it down from a child's point of view can really help you understand what you are holding on to.

Grab a pencil and some paper, take a seat in your physical space, and trigger the anchor you set to enter your mental space. Breathe and be present in this peaceful moment. Ask your inner child if they'd like to write you a letter. If they say no, don't force the issue and try again another day.

If they say yes, tell them you have a pencil and paper ready for what they have to say. With your *non-dominant* hand, start writing whatever comes to mind. Allow your mind to write freely. Don't be surprised if your handwriting isn't very clear or if you doodle or even write anywhere but in the lines. Let them write for as long as they want to.

Understand that some children are far less communicative than others. It might not go exactly to plan, but the purpose is to give them freedom—not to force it. Allow whatever happens to happen.

Write what comes to you, no matter what it is. Allow your inner child to express themselves through you. They have waited so long for someone to listen. When you finish writing, take a moment and "return" to your adult self. Stand up and give your body a little shake to help you physically and mentally return to the present moment.

Now, as an adult, read the letter you wrote. Don't judge it or criticize it. Read it and soak it in. Keep this letter in your journal or any safe place. Come back to it as often as you need. You may discover some valuable insights as a response to this exercise.

EXERCISE: PLAYDATE WITH YOUR INNER CHILD

Children are naturally playful and inquisitive, and it's time for you to encourage that for yourself. Reparenting can often feel like work on both parts of you, so set some time aside for play.

As adults, we have a list of reasons we can't slow down and enjoy ourselves. It may look like, "I can relax once the house is totally clean," or "I'll have time for play once this project is turned in at work." However, when we deny ourselves regular time to play, we set ourselves up for burnout. There will *always* be a reason to put off having fun, and there will always be work to do, but you don't need to earn rest.

You want to find something that you and your inner child can enjoy. So, it's probably not driving around shopping, running errands, or something 'adult.' Consider something like finger paints, playing with clay, drawing, grabbing an ice cream sundae, or swinging on a swing set.

You have *one* job in this exercise, and that's to have fun! If you get an "idea" in the middle of playing, listen to it. It's most likely your inner child's creativity and imagination coming out to play. It's okay to listen to these ideas and try something new. Maybe it's coloring a pirate ship yellow. Maybe it's shooting down a slide face-first. Maybe it's creating a giant octopus with Play-Doh. Whatever it is, have fun with it. Make sure that the fun activity you choose is something that a child may want to experience. Here's a list of things you can try:

- skipping rope
- drawing
- playing on a playground
- blowing bubbles
- making up a fantasy story about penguins and pirates
- interviewing a cat and giving it a voice to talk back
- making a treasure map
- pretending the floor is lava

For more great ideas, visit the bonus resources at www.vitalskillspress.com/innerchild-resources. Leave your adult self in the car. Really! Don't bring any planning or judgment on this exercise. This is about letting loose and getting in touch with being a kid again. A lot of times, our adult brains can ruin the fun by attempting to justify or control what's happening. Let the activity unfold how it will. No plans and no holding back.

EXERCISE: RESOLVING INTERNAL CONFLICT

In Chapter 2, we asked out inner child if they would be willing to speak with us and identified that part within us. This exercise builds on the concept of discovering conflicting parts and can help resolve conflict in any situation. For now, we will build on the foundation we created earlier.

A quick recap: we often refer to the *parts of us* in regular speech. Sometimes you may say "there's a part of me that wants to do something, and another part that wants to do something different." These are *the parts* we identified in chapter 2.

Once you've identified each part and asked if they are willing talk, we need to begin the conflict resolution.

First, move each part so it's like the part is sitting in the upward-facing palm of your hand.

Then, one at a time, ask each part to explain what its problem is. Don't interrupt it or make any judgments or conclusions.

You've most likely done a similar exercise without knowing about it if you've ever said, "On one hand, I want to do X, but on the other, I want to do Y."

Once you've heard both sides, ask the first part, "What is the positive intention of your actions?"

A positive intention is the reason a part of you acts the way it does. No matter what the behavior is, it has a positive intention. To find the real intention, ask, "So what does that give you?" until you get to the bottom layer of reasoning.

Every part has a role to play in keeping us safe, happy, and healthy. There is no such thing as an inner enemy. No part is intentionally trying to sabotage you. Maybe, if you ask the part what its positive intention is, it's trying to *protect* you.

As a note, the positive intention of the part does not mean the action is the best way to fulfill the intention. It's simply a means of understanding what is at the heart of the behavior.

When both sides have their positive intention, ask each part, "Can you see how this other part is trying to help?" and "Are you willing to work with the other part to help it achieve the positive intentions of both parts?"

If the parts agree with each other, you can move on to the next step. If they don't agree, continue to ask the part that doesn't agree on what it needs to help the other part achieve its goal. This is only likely if you don't initially get down to the core positive intention.

With total part agreement, turn your palms to face each other and slowly bring them toward each other. Don't force this action. Move as slowly as you need for both parts to feel comfortable. If there is resistance, slow the movement. If the resistance continues, ask what else needs to happen for both parties to integrate and work with each other.

When the resistance disappears, resume slowly, bringing your hands together. Once your hands have come together, interlace your fingers and hold them like that in front of you for a few seconds.

Bring your clasped hands to your chest and integrate your parts back into your body.

Finally, it's time to do a "system-wide check" and make sure everything in your body feels congruent and okay with the compromise that was created. If something feels off or uncomfortable, ask that part to show itself and repeat the process with the new part.

The goal of this exercise is to create harmony and understanding between two conflicting parts while respecting that each part has a critical role to play in your life.

6

MASTER YOUR EMOTIONS

When we honor our inner child's feelings, we release the emotional hurts that we're still subconsciously carrying around.

— PATRICIA HOPE

Kathy was sound asleep in her bed until she was startled awake by a thunder crack so deep it shook her room. The wind howled so fiercely it slammed the shutter into her window, cracking the top left corner before ripping it right off.

As a 7 year old, Kathy had never experienced a raging gale-force storm in the middle of the night before, and this one was brutal. She couldn't tak it anymore and ran screaming to her parents' room, looking for comfort.

From that night on, Kathy hated storms. The thunder would make her curl up into a ball and hold her hands over her ears. Even the little ones that blew by in the daytime. Her fear grew with anything that sounded like a storm. Fireworks, loud car exhausts, gunfire, and even trains chugging down the tracks.

Nearly 40 years later, after the fateful storm was not even a blip in Kathy's memory, loud noises sent her into a full-blown panic attack.

Kathy couldn't control her instant emotional reaction to any loud noise. So, she built her life around quiet places. Small towns, libraries, and coffee shops were Kathy's happy places. One day, her boss needed to send her to headquarters in the heart of downtown Manhattan for an important meeting with one of the company's top clients. It was Kathy's worst nightmare. Afraid of a panic attack, or worse, Kathy could only think of one way to fix this pending nightmare. She quit. She left an amazing job because she couldn't bring herself to face her biggest fear or get a handle on her emotions for even a quick business trip.

EMOTIONS OF CHILDHOOD

You might not actively remember the emotions you felt in childhood. Many of us don't remember very far back in our childhood at all. For me, my earliest memory is about five, and even that is only a piece of a memory with additional detail added from talking about it with my parents. Many of my memories don't really start until about eight or nine. The older we get, the less likely it is that we can actively remember all the details of our childhood. Still, that doesn't change the fact that what you felt in your younger years affects you *now*.

Children experience the same complex emotions we do as adults, but most don't have a wide understanding or vocabulary to express their emotions. From birth until about five, we experience the five basic emotions: mad, glad, sad, lonely, and scared. More complex emotions develop, and we discover anger, anxiety, guilt, shame, love, surprise, and excitement, to name a few[40].

Just because a child experiences these emotions doesn't mean they know how to communicate them or even what to do with their emotions. When that happens, frustration sets in. If that frustration continues, it creates an emotional wound that the body holds on to, sometimes forever, if it's not dealt with. Emotional wounds are what's left after an uncomfortable or unpleasant experience.

Unfortunately, emotional wounds don't fade away with time. Even where we can't recall an experience, we still carry the damage with us. The powerful emotions that we felt as a child—anxiety, fear, shame—are still felt in our bodies, even decades later[30].

THE SCIENCE OF EMOTIONS

All emotions can be broken down into five steps.

- Step 1: an event
- Step 2: filtering.
- Step 3: subjective experience
- Step 4: a physiological response
- Step 5: a behavioral response

An Event

Every emotion begins with an event. It includes the facts of the event with no emotions involved. Imagine experiencing a Ground Plank Rigenshaffer for the first time. Since you've never experienced this before *(I know because I just made the word up)*, you have no emotions associated with the experience yet. You're interacting with pure reality, as you have nothing to compare it with or an experience to pull from.

No matter what you do in life, every experience you have has a base truth. There is an actual event that happens with no emotion tied to it. Meeting your mother for dinner, cleaning your shoes, driving to the dentist, it doesn't matter. The event itself has no emotions.

Filtering

At the exact moment you interact with reality, your brain filters it through your past experiences. This is a survival mechanism our brains developed over thousands of years. All experience is filtered through your five senses: sight, sound, touch, taste, and smell.

The first thing that 'disappears' in your experience is smell. How often can you remember smells with all your memories? For some memories, it's very important; for many, it's not. That's why when you first get into a new car, you can smell the brand-new leather. But by the time you've finished the test drive, you can't 'smell' the leather anymore. Your brain filters that information out because it's not important at the moment.

Much like the smell, other pieces of information about the event are filtered. Your past experiences create an expectation for almost everything you encounter throughout the day. You hit every red light on a certain road no matter what time of day you drive it. Your father always judges you and expects more from you. The rain brings gloomy feelings. You get the point.

Your filter only accepts the information you know to be true. Now, what's interesting is when your filter experiences something that doesn't match what it believes.

Let's say your filter says you're bad at math. This is common, especially among women. But you can probably look at a bank statement and easily figure out how the balance was calculated.

Money in, money out. You don't need to understand the math behind the interest to add it to your balance. So, if you can do addition and subtraction, you're not actually bad at math. You may just believe that you are, so you filter out any experience that works to prove your belief wrong.

This is why two people can have the same physical experience but remember the event differently.

Subjective Experience

Since your filter is always working actively, you no longer interact with true reality but with your version of reality. This is your subjective experience. Your subjective experience triggers your emotional response.

A coffee date with your mother has a lot of history that comes with it. Your filter kicks in, and you have a subjective experience. Your mother asked, "How's your month been? It feels like forever since I've seen you."

Maybe you have a great relationship with your mother, and you've had a busy travel month, so you excitedly catch her up on all the places you've seen. Maybe you have a strained relationship with your mother, so you feel judged because you haven't called her in a while, and she keeps harping on about when you're going to give her grandkids.

It's this step where emotions begin.

Physiological Response

Your emotions live in your body. When they show up, you feel them in different areas. A tightness in your chest, a pit in your stomach, a lump in your throat, sweaty palms, the list goes on. These responses are involuntary and are controlled by your autonomic nervous system. The autonomic nervous system is also in control of our fight-or-flight response which we discussed back in chapter 4. It plays a significant role in our evolutionary development and survival.

Your emotions trigger your body to prepare for fight or flight. That's why an emotion of happiness can have a relaxing feeling with it. The emotion of anger brings blood pumping into your muscles and increases your adrenaline. In the event you need to act quickly, your body prepares itself for the action.

Behavioral Response

This is when you express emotion. This can include smiling, crying, balling your fists, or shouting. How you express your emotions is different for everyone. Your behavioral responses are there to express to the world how you feel in a moment.

THE POWER OF NAMING EMOTIONS

Can you name your emotions? Actually, a better question would be, how many emotions can you name? Happy, sad, angry, frustrated, surprised, disgusted? Did you know that there are upwards of 34,000 identified emotions[21]? It's no wonder that even as adults, we struggle to name what we're feeling.

Why is it important to put a name to our emotions? Psychologists at the University of California, Los Angeles (UCLA)[37] put this question to the test. They asked 88 people with a fear of spiders to get as close as they could to a live tarantula. They were asked to walk close enough to touch it if they could. Their study tested one thing. What happens if you label your emotions?

After being asked to approach a tarantula, the participants were divided into groups and brought to a room with another live tarantula in a container. The first group was asked to describe the emotions they experienced and label their reactions. They would say things like, "I'm anxious and frightened by the terrifying spider."

The second group was asked to use neutral terms that did not talk about their fear. This approach was to change the experience and make it less threatening. Participants would say, "That spider can't hurt me. I'm not afraid of it."

The third group was told to talk about things that had nothing to do with their experience. The last group was not told to say anything. They were just exposed to the spider.

One week later, the participants were re-exposed to the tarantula outside and asked to get as close as they could and possibly touch it with their fingers. The researchers measured how close the participants got, how distressed they were, and the sweat on their palms both times.

Their research showed that the group who labeled their emotions did significantly better than the other three. They got much closer than the last two groups and a little closer than the second group. Their hands produced significantly less sweat than all other participants.

This study shows the power of naming emotions. It gives you power over your responses and helps you to bring your feelings and emotions under control. When you take the step from "I am..." to "I am feeling..." you consciously bring awareness to the fact that you are *not* your emotions. You simply feel them.

So, if naming our emotions helps us to handle situations, but there are literally thousands of emotions we can feel, where do we start? As with most things, we start a little at a time.

Pick one moment in your life, like right now, for example, and name the emotion you're feeling. Right now. What is it? Content, peace, joy, calm? Whatever it is, give it a name. This is the beginning of becoming self-aware and the start of regaining emotional control.

EMOTIONAL CONTROL—WHY IS IT NECESSARY?

Very few people I know enjoy being out of control. If you think of when you last had that feeling, I'll bet it centered on an intense emotion, like anger. When we experience intense feelings, the idea of controlling our emotions may seem farfetched. However, you probably already have some level of emotional control, even if you aren't consciously aware of it.

Do you listen to calming music when you are feeling anxious? What about counting to ten when you're feeling yourself mad? Or going for a run to let off some steam? Anything you do to help balance your emotions is emotional control.

The ability to regulate your emotions is the key to mental well-being. When your emotions are more intense, you are more likely to make unreasonable or irrational decisions. For example, had you not listened to calming music to dampen your nerves, you might have made a snap decision in a panic to quit your job even if there was a better solution to solve your problem. When we give ourselves time to come down from intense emotions, we create a buffer. This buffer is where we can honor our emotions and how a situation makes us feel without allowing our feelings to rule our decisions and reactions. If you make a snap decision and yell at someone in an emotional state, you might do more damage than the initial event warranted.

For Kathy, her snap decision caused her to quit a job she loved. This created significant financial hardship for her. I ended a friendship over something as silly as a cat. My emotions got the better of me because an old roommate brought home a cat. I was furious. Not only did she not ask if I wanted to have a pet, but our lease also didn't allow animals in the apartments. To add to it, she wasn't really around all that often, which made the responsibility fall on me. In my anger, I packed up all my things and moved out overnight. I said nothing to her. I just left. To this day, I haven't really talked to her. I ended the relationship because of my anger.

Now, I'm not telling you that emotional control means to dismiss your emotions or the situation. But, if I had controlled my emotions and given myself a buffer to think through things with a little more clarity, I may have saved the relationship or come up with a better solution than running away and giving up.

There are several ways for us to work through our emotions, and at the end of this chapter, I'll provide a few to help you get started.

EMOTIONAL INTELLIGENCE

Emotional intelligence is the ability to perceive, control, and evaluate emotions. It helps you navigate social situations with more ease and a better understanding of yourself.

Emotional intelligence is especially important to interpersonal relationships. It helps us operate with empathy and understanding for the people we interact with. Emotional intelligence helps us know how to respond when someone is struggling, how to navigate a social gathering where tensions are running high, and when a situation is getting out of control before we have lost our ability to remain calm[36].

Self-Awareness

We must first be aware of how we show emotions before we can change the way we react. According to the Oxford Dictionary, self-awareness is "conscious knowledge of one's character, feelings, motives, and desires". It is the ability to focus on yourself and identify how your actions and thoughts align with your standards. Self-awareness provides you with the ability to evaluate yourself objectively, regulate your emotions, and understand how others might perceive you. You are better able to interpret your own thoughts and actions through an objective lens.

Self-awareness is the first step in managing your emotions. It is no good to know what you're doing if you don't have a goal in mind for how you want to act. You likely know several people who are very aware of how they come across and choose not to do anything about it. They may also use their awareness as an excuse to act a certain way.

Self-Regulation

I used to work with a guy who would always answer a request with no. It didn't matter what the request was. Do you want to grab a bite to eat? 'No.' Can we adjust the order button color to orange? 'No.' Would you like an extra day to think about something big? 'No.' Pete operated in constant fear. Any change, big or little, would send him into a spiral of doom. It didn't help that he was the director of marketing in our company. He was resistant to change in any capacity. What we were doing worked, and there was no reason to change anything.

When I asked him about this, he constantly said, "You know I don't like change. It scares me." Well, let's give him one for being aware of his emotions, but true emotional intelligence isn't just about being aware of your emotions. It's about learning how to manage them.

Now, imagine how much faster the company could grow if, for a moment, Pete could put aside his fear and work through his sometimes very valid concerns from a place of calm. The people involved could help create a robust testing method, and we would have been able to catch issues early because of Pete's ability to find where everything could go wrong. That seems like a much more effective way to handle the situation, but instead, Pete lets his fear run his decisions.

To develop emotional intelligence, you must learn to control and regulate your emotions. It doesn't mean putting them on lockdown. It merely means waiting for the right time and place to express those emotions. A tantrum in the grocery store isn't the best time *or* place, and neither is a blowup at the office over the copier being jammed. Instead, having yourself a good cry at home or journaling can be a much better way to handle the building emotions.

Motivation

Who do you want to be and why? This is the essence of emotional intelligence. If you don't have a clear picture of who you want to be, then how will you know how to react? Take a moment or three and dream of the best version of yourself. Give yourself free rein to model this image with all your hopes, dreams, and motivations.

In the first chapter, we created a detailed vision of our safe mental place. This is the time to put all your details into who you want to be or, better yet, who you are becoming.

We used to dream of who we would be as children. These would often be impressive people: astronauts, firefighters, the President of the United States, a ballerina, or something else entirely. We played like we were these amazing people. Over the years, we lost the dream, or we lost the vision of who we wanted to be.

Now, we have the chance to define this person anew. Who do you want to become? What do they look like? How do they act? What is their dominant emotional state? How do they react in tough situations? What do they sound like? What are some phrases this person may say? How do they dress? What hobbies do they enjoy? The more detail you put into the idea of who you are becoming, the better.

You can incorporate this with a dream board, a vision board, or simply writing a description of your future self on paper. But the goal is to get a clear understanding of where you are going.

Next, we define the why behind your desired change. Your why keeps you going when times get tough. The best way to discover your why is to answer a sequence of questions. "Why do I want to become this person?" "Why is that important to me?" Keep asking yourself the last question until your answers repeat themselves. Now you have a solid why.

With your vision of who you are becoming and your why in place, you have a great roadmap to help you navigate and change your emotional reactions. The person I am becoming is someone who enjoys being healthy. They use exercise as a way of working through tough emotions and big decisions. Why? Because I want to be around to see and enjoy my grandkids and great-grandkids. So, when I have a particularly frustrating day, I look forward to blowing off some steam on my rowing machine. When I have to make a big decision for work, my business, or with my kids, I look forward to spending some personal time on my rower to attack the decision from all angles. The person I am becoming takes this necessary time before making emotional decisions. They use the phrases, "I'll let you know tomorrow" and "I need a day to think this over" when necessary.

Self-Reflection

As we grow in our emotional intelligence, we may question why we act a certain way or why something triggers an emotion. We often do this naturally. "Why did I get so worked up?" "Why did that text from my ex bring me to tears?" Why, why, why.

There's a difference behind defining *why we want to do something* as we did in the previous section, and asking *why we currently do things* that may not be the most helpful.

The problem with why when evaluating current action is that it puts us and others on the defensive. "Why would you do that?" feels very accusatory. When we're dealing with other people, we can change the temperature of a conversation quickly without meaning to when asking why.

A better question to ask is, "What?" This question gives us information that we can use to change an outcome. "What caused you to do that?" will get you much farther in a conflict than "Why would you do that?" The question *what* is exploratory? It allows you and the other person to understand an issue or an emotion without feeling attacked. "*What*" can help us remove our emotions from the evaluation of the situation. It allows us to think objectively about what is going on and what causes our emotional reactions.

Empathy

Empathy is the ability to understand the emotions of others and put yourself in their shoes. It allows you to see something from another person's perspective. This does not mean you take on the other person's emotions, but simply that you understand the emotions they have.

When my youngest child experiences big emotions, he is very sharp with his words. For a while, the response in my house was, "That sounds like a you problem." Which, as you might suspect, did nothing to help the emotions of his situation. It was a rather dismissive and downright rude response. It also showed zero empathy for his feelings. Now, we handle things a little differently. We start by acknowledging the way we think he is feeling and then giving him the chance to talk about it. "It sounds like you might be upset. And when you say mean things to me, it makes me upset. How can we work through this together?"

We're being empathetic because we're recognizing his feelings. We're not taking them on as our own feelings, but we're giving him the space to have his emotions and working through them together.

As adults, we can understand where someone is coming from. Maybe they had a hard day at work. Maybe they have something stressful going on at home. Either way, when we give other people the space to experience their emotions without judgment, we can understand what's really going on.

Empathy for others is the last stage of emotional intelligence because it involves people outside yourself. We don't want to use empathy to change someone else. That's manipulation. Instead, when we have empathy for others because we have good emotional control over our own emotions, we have better relationships all around.

EXERCISE: EMOTIONAL AWARENESS JOURNALING PROMPTS

When writing in a journal, it's best to let your writing flow. Don't hold back or censor what your hands want to write. The following prompts will help get you started on the journey of emotional awareness and control.

- What has been bothering me a lot lately?
- What do I have control over, and what do I *not* have control over regarding [insert problem here]?
- What emotions have I been feeling a lot lately, and where do I feel them in my body?
- What emotions do I find the hardest to accept?
- What emotion would I like to explore more?
- When do I feel the strongest emotions?
- What triggers my powerful emotions?
- Instead of feeling _____, I would rather feel _____, because_____
- What is one emotional challenge I faced today?
- What strengths did I rely on to keep me focused on the best version of myself?
- Who am I becoming, and why?

EXERCISE: POSITIVE OUTCOMES AND FUTURE PACING

A positive outcome is what we expect and how we will act from a situation or goal state. Future pacing is the art of testing and playing out a scenario in the future. The combination of the two helps us to live in a way consistent with the type of person we want to be. It helps us to keep our emotions in check and can prepare us for an event before we need to have it in real life.

To start, think about a situation or a scenario you might experience in the future if you want to have better control over your emotions. This could be a simple interaction with an ex, an email you must write letting go of one of your employees, an interview for a new job, or a move across town.

Once you have the situation you want to work on, let's grab a seat in our physical space and prepare to enter our mental space.

First, we must create the positive outcome we want, defined in the way we want to see it happen, the way we want to feel, and what we will hear. Outcomes are based on sensory experiences, just like our emotions.

Next, answer the following questions to create your outcome.

- What specifically do you want?
- What will having that do for you?

These questions are stated in the positive. *I want to feel confident in groups. I want to feel a sense of calm when communicating with my partner.* Notice none of the examples said, "I don't want." *I don't want to cry when I'm angry* is not an example of a positive outcome. It's okay to start with what you don't want and then decide what you want. If you don't want to cry, what do you want instead?

- When, where, how, and with whom do you want it?

Not all outcomes are appropriate in all situations. So, define when your outcome is relevant.

- What stops you from having what you want?
- What do you need to achieve this outcome?

There are times when we need additional training to achieve what we want. We may need to anchor a resource we haven't used in a while. (The anchoring exercise we completed in Chapter 2 is handy for accessing these types of resources.)

- Is this outcome only for you?

We can only control ourselves. We cannot control others. Our outcomes must be rooted in what we have control over. *I want John to see things my way,* which is not an outcome we can control. Instead, what resources do we have control over that can help influence the situation? *I want to stay calm and clear when I talk with John* about us and our reaction.

- What will you gain or lose with this outcome?

No matter what our outcome is, we will lose something, and we will gain something. When we identify what that is, we ensure the outcome is really something we want. For example, if I want to be calm in all my interactions with my ex, I stand to lose spinning out of control and emotional outbursts. I stand to gain peace of mind and energy, as I don't spend a lot of time on emotions that don't serve me.

When you have the answer to all these questions, you have a good, positive outcome. Now, we can test this outcome with some future pacing.

Imagine a specific event based on your outcome that will happen soon. Based on your outcome, how do you act? What do you feel? What do you see? How do you conduct yourself?

Consider the future pacing a trial run of who you want to be. If you don't initially like the way it plays out in your mind, what additional resources do you need? What part of your outcome do you need or want to change? Is there something that was missing? Or is it something you need to remove from the situation?

Rework your outcome to adjust for what was missing, and then imagine the event again.

Now that you've done this exercise, when the event happens, you'll notice you have a lot more emotional control over the situation because you've already experienced it before. And you've trained your body to act the way you want instead of the way you used to react, which wasn't successful for you in the past.

EXERCISE: NAMING YOUR EMOTIONS

It's overwhelming to get started with understanding all the emotions a person can experience. That's where an emotion wheel can be handy. You can access the wheel of emotions from www.vitalskillspress.com/innerchild-resources

To get started, we first identify the core emotion we have. Core emotions are sadness, anger, happiness, fear, and disgust. Every emotion we can feel stems from one and sometimes two of these emotions.

Once you have your core emotion identified, it's time to narrow it down a little further. Let's say your core emotion is fear. From here, you might narrow it down to feeling humiliated, rejected, insecure, anxious, or scared. We can go another step deeper. If you're anxious, you might be worried or overwhelmed. When we have a deeper understanding of our emotions, we can figure out what we need to do to help control our emotions.

From here, you have two avenues you can go. One is to keep your current emotion, and the other is to decide if you want to change your emotion. If you don't feel your emotions are resourceful for you now, you have a potential plan of action to adjust your emotions.

If you identify being overwhelmed, are there areas you can get help or things you can move off your plate? If you identified being worried, there may be things you can do to ease your worry. Either way, once you know what the real emotion you're feeling, you can develop the roadmap to unpack it and change or adjust it as needed.

7
WHO ARE YOU BECOMING?

A dream written down with a date becomes a goal. A goal broken down into steps becomes a plan. A plan backed by action makes your dreams come true.

— GREG REID

WHO DO YOU WANT TO BE?

Throughout the whole book, we've been talking about how to investigate the past to heal. Now, we're going to integrate everything together and work to create a better, brighter future. This is when we get to work with our inner child to design the type of person we choose to be.

We've suffered in silence long enough. We've been conditioned to keep our emotions and feelings to ourselves. Now is the time to break free. Don't worry, we'll do it in steps. You do as many or as little as you feel comfortable doing along the way.

Life of Design vs Life of Happenstance

When I first started down the path of designing the life I wanted, I had a really hard time. My coach asked me, "Where do you see yourself in five years?" My friends asked, "What do you want to do?" No matter what question was asked, my answer was always, "I don't know." Worse, I could tell them what my husband wanted, but I literally did not know what I wanted.

Well, by definition, that means I could get whatever was given to me, and I'd be happy. I didn't know what I wanted, and I got really uncomfortable when people would push the issue. The more questions they asked me about what I wanted, the more defensive and angrier I got. Why? Because I was mad at myself for not knowing.

Let's say you're looking for a place to live. There are 195 different countries in the world. Okay, maybe you know you want to live in the United States, but where? There are 50 states and over 14 territories. This creates an overwhelming number of options for you to pick from. This can be scary.

Let's say you know the city and state you want to live in. Let's suppose you even know the zip code you want to live in. There are still a lot of options available to you. Your realtor will have a hard time doing their job of showing you the right place, and even worse, you won't even know when the right place comes along because you don't know what you want.

Unfortunately, this happens with nearly everything in our life.

So, let's begin by asking yourself what you want. It is okay if you don't know yet. Write "What do I want?" on a piece of paper. Take 10 minutes and think about this question. Write anything that comes to mind. Don't worry if it's silly. Don't worry if it's too far out there. Don't worry if it seems simple. Just write whatever comes to mind.

If you're having a hard time with this, I understand. For everyone who struggles with what they want, it's okay. I know exactly what that feels like.

Now, take a *new* piece of paper out and write "what I don't want" at the top of the page. Draw a line down the middle of the paper. On the left side of the paper, list everything you don't want. Again, don't censor yourself. Whatever you think of, write it down.

Take 10 minutes and do this exercise. Not only can it be a little cathartic and freeing, but it removes the negativity from our heads and puts it on paper. From here, we can shape it and do something about it. If you're on a roll with writing, don't stop. Get everything down on the paper in front of you.

Once you've finished, you will have two pages. One with what you want and the other half filled with what you don't want. Which list is longer? This isn't a judgment. It's your starting point. Congratulations. We must know where we are before we can decide where we want to go.

The last step of this exercise is to take the list of what you don't want and ask yourself the following question: *If I don't want this, what do I want instead?* Write what you *do* want the right-hand column.

For example, if you don't want to cry every time you have to step into your boss's office, what do you want instead? For me, I wanted to step in with calm confidence. If you don't want to weigh 250 pounds, what do you want instead? I wanted to be 150 pounds.

This may take a few minutes. If you're ahead of the game here, you may realize that what you want can change. And that's the beauty of this. Yes, what you want can, and often does, change over time. So, this shouldn't be a one-and-done kind of exercise. This way, you can constantly adjust to what your life looks like as you grow into who you want to be.

One final thought. There is no such thing as better; there's only a tradeoff. What works for you may not work for someone else, and that's okay. By saying 'no' to something, you're saying "yes" to something else and vice versa. It's when we get intentional about what we say yes or no to that we start to feel control over our lives.

Be Kind to Yourself

One of my core beliefs is "there's no such thing as an inner enemy." Everything that happens in your life, everything that you think, every way you react, and every way you behave serve you. You are not out to sabotage yourself. There isn't a part of you that's working against your greater good.

Yes, that means that even the voice inside that may tell you that you're not good enough isn't trying to sabotage you. There is always, and I mean always, a positive intention behind what's going on. For many women, the underlying positive intention may be safety and security. It's why you'll often see survivors of sexual abuse put on weight. This happens because deep down, there's a part of them that feels that excess weight will make them unattractive to people[36]. Or it could be a literal physical barrier their body is trying to create. The excess weight is a safety and security mechanism of the part that was hurt and abused.

When we understand this fundamental truth, we can then look at all our behaviors and break them down to their core. When you find the core desire, it's easy to understand why you may react the way you are. Now, you have the baseline of compassion for yourself.

I've said it before, and I'll say it again. You and your inner child have gotten you through 100% of the situations you've been through. So, as we go through the process of deciding what you want your life to be, it's important to remember to be kind to yourself about where you are.

Years ago, I was talking to my best friend. I constantly berated and belittled myself. "I'm so stupid. I'm an idiot. I can't believe I could be such a failure." Sometimes, I would do it to be funny. Other times, I would do it to take the feeling of guilt away from the issue. One day, my best friend stopped me dead in my tracks and said, "Hey, don't talk about my friend like that. She's a really cool person I like to hang out with." It was a punch in the gut with how badly I talked about and treated myself.

We seem to have an endless amount of compassion for everyone around us, but we don't give ourselves the same treatment. Have you ever said you are your own worst critic? Or maybe I'm harsher on myself than anyone else is? Why do you think that is? If you wouldn't let someone you love say negative things about themselves, it's time to turn that compassion inward and show yourself a little kindness.

There are three major components to show yourself compassion.

1. **Kindness versus judgment.** There will always be slip-ups and obstacles. Those who are kind to themselves can be gentle and understanding, realizing that we can't always be exactly who we want to be. We are not robots.

We are perfectly imperfect. Judgments are when we take an action or emotion and criticize them. Everyone has flaws, and everyone makes mistakes. It's okay to be kind to yourself as you work to become the person you want to be.
2. **Humanity versus isolation.** You are not alone in your journey and your experiences. I bet you could pick five random people off the street, and they would have similar negative emotions and critical thoughts about themselves. We are not isolated. Humans pretty much all have the same ways they talk and think about themselves. Keep this in mind the next time you think you're the only one who is hard on yourself.
3. **Mindfulness versus identification.** Mindfulness is a state of awareness. It's when you can take your emotions and actions for what they are. You are not your emotions. If you can separate your identity from your emotions, you can see how your thoughts, emotions, and behaviors are all adjustable and not the definition of who you are.

Create a Support System

You are on your own journey, but you don't have to do it alone. Find people who will help support you as you grow into the person you want to be. This can be a group of girlfriends you see once a month or an accountability partner you talk to once a week. It can be your family, or it can be someone you've not yet met. The goal is to bring people into your life who can help you become the best version of yourself.

The more proximity you give to people, the more influence they have on your life. This means the more you hang out with someone, the more you're likely to become just like them. While the concept is simple, it's not always easy.

Start small. Invite someone into your life who supports the change you're looking to make. This could be a fitness trainer if you're trying to lose weight. It could be a therapist if you're looking to work through some mental struggles. It could be someone who is good at a new hobby you want to try.

As you surround yourself with the people you want in your life, you can restrict access to the people you don't want in your life. If you have a set of friends who treat you the way you don't want to be treated, reduce their access to you. You can skip the next 'girls' night' because you have an appointment with yourself. You have a competing event in your new hobby that would make it difficult to hang out with a toxic family member. Removing people from your life can feel drastic. If you don't want to start out with drastic measures, reduce their access to you first.

The more support you have from people who believe in your dream and who you are becoming, the easier it is for you to become that person. The right people can inspire you; the wrong people can drag you down. Choose wisely.

ALIGNMENT OF NEUROLOGICAL LEVELS

Have you ever felt stuck at a job and thought, "If I change jobs, this would be so much better?" Only to change jobs and find out that you have the same problem at the new job? Or maybe you've thought, "I can't stand my gym *(or insert any physical place you go to)*. I'll go to a different one and get away from the negativity." Then, when you find the new place, you discover the same issues.

Another one I see happen often is switching out a significant other. "My ex always did this thing I didn't like, so I got a new one. But they do the same thing!" We often feel it's our lot in life to suffer with the same issues over and over, no matter where we are.

Why does this happen? Is the same problem at both jobs? Is the same issue at both gyms? Are the different people we've been with all the same?

Probably not. The biggest issue is we're trying to change something at the wrong neurological level. What's a neurological level? It is a hierarchy of levels for change. Much like Maslow's hierarchy of needs, the neurological levels stack on top of each other and affect each other[6].

The neurological levels are environment, behavior, capability, beliefs, identity, and spirit. They are arranged from easiest to change to most difficult. As you move up in the levels, the time required to change also increases. Let's examine each one a little closer.

Environment

This is the physical representation of everything around you. Where you live, how your house is laid out, what clothes you wear, the people you see, your job, your significant other, everything.

When I first started my business, I had my desk facing the wall. I would sit down at my computer and stare at a wall. The room was open behind me, and my door was at my back. Anyone could walk in on me, and I wouldn't notice. That's exactly what my ex-husband used to do to me. He loved to startle me. So, he would creep into my office without making a sound, trying to get as close to me as he could without me noticing. Then he would touch me on my shoulder or say something right next to my ear, and it would make me jump out of my skin.

I absolutely hated it, but he would laugh uncontrollably every time.

One day, I completely redecorated my office. I turned my desk around so I was facing into the room instead of the wall. I put the window to my back and could easily see the door. This time, when he tried to enter my room, I met him with a cheery "Hello." I removed his ability to scare me by simply rearranging my environment. It was a simple fix and saved my nerves.

Your environment is easy to change. Move cities. Change your home. Work at a new job. They're all easy fixes to a problem, but not all problems are fixed so easily. If you've made a change to your environment and the problem still exists, it's time to move up a neurological level.

Behaviors

This is what we do, consciously or not. It's the patterns and habits we've built. There are some changes that must happen at the behavioral level. If I changed gym multiple times, changed trainers, changed workout routines, and changed workout clothes multiple times but still have weight I'm trying to lose, it's most likely a behavior issue that's getting in the way.

If every time I want to go to the gym, I hit the snooze button instead, no amount of gym changes is going to fix the problem. If, after every great workout, I eat a Big Mac and Supersize fries, no amount of workout routine is going to fix the problem. My issue lies in the behavioral realm.

Joanne used to be someone who didn't wake up with her first alarm. She tried everything, like switching the ringer, getting an obnoxious "old-school" alarm with the external bells, and setting five alarms in a row going off every two minutes. She even tried the one that vibrates the bed to wake her up, but nothing seemed to work. She slept through or hit the snooze enough times to be late. Every. Single. Day.

Joanne's issue wasn't environment-based. It was solely her behavior. Every night, she drank energy drinks at 8 pm, right before she jumped online to log in and game for hours with her friends. She'd only get about four hours of sleep before her alarm went off, and she had to be up for work. Now, sure, you may think the answer is obvious. Go to bed earlier, stop drinking energy drinks so late, and adjust when she needs to be at work. There are several things she can do to fix the issue. Every single one of them is behavior in nature. So, if she changes her behavior, she has a better chance of getting the results she wants.

Some behaviors are so deeply rooted in our lives that it's hard to change them. That's why making small, incremental changes helps. You can find a list of resources that I have used over the years to make behavior and habit changes at www.vitalskillspress.com/innerchild-resources.

Capabilities

The next neurological level is your capabilities or skills. These are your skills and natural talents and can fall into one of four categories.

1. **You know what you know**. You are certain you know these. These range from as simple as breathing and walking to as complex as surgery if you know how to

perform such an operation. This is the first category of capabilities that we are consciously aware of.

2. **You know what you don't know**. I, personally, don't know how to perform surgery of any kind. So, this skill falls squarely into the category of knowledge that I don't know. This is the second category of capabilities that we are consciously aware of.
3. **You don't know what you know**. Have you ever done something for the first time and were pretty good at it? It may have even made you say, "I didn't know I could do that!" These are skills you didn't even know you had.
4. **You don't know what you don't know**. These are skills you don't know about, and they are not even in your world of possibility of knowing. At least, not until you meet someone who can bring the understanding of these skills into your circle of awareness. Skills can move from here into any of the other categories by realizing what you don't know.

Every single one of your skills and capabilities falls into one of these categories. Sometimes, our problems can be solved by upgrading or learning a new capability. For many of you reading this book, you may or may not have known about some skills for talking to and healing your inner child. Now you do, and you can take those new skills and use them to see new and different results in your life. When you bump up against a problem that isn't solved by environment or behavior, take a step back and see if there is a skill you need to gain.

Beliefs and Values

Beliefs and values are the things that drive us at a deep level. They are what you hold most dear and important and help to provide direction for what you want in life.

If you have a value of honesty, you may believe that telling the truth is important. If you believe this, you will tell the truth even when faced with a difficult or uncomfortable situation.

Your values and beliefs can be on the conscious or subconscious level. This means there are some values and beliefs you are aware of and some you are not.

You may have a belief that you are bad at math. This means every time you're presented with a math problem, you instantly feel a tightness in your chest and stare at the problem blankly. The numbers may not even make sense to you.

So, even if you take classes to learn math and carry a calculator around with you (capability and behavior), you may still struggle with math problems because you believe you are bad at math.

There's good news. You aren't stuck with these beliefs and values any more than you're stuck with anything else we've talked about so far. However, updating them takes time. It takes more time than simply changing your environment, but it can be done.

To start, define your values. I have a deck of value cards I revisit every year. I have personal values, family values, values for my business, and even product values. If you don't have a deck of cards, you can do a quick search to get a list of values. I go through my deck of cards and pull out any value that I like, want, or wish to develop for whatever it is I'm working on. When you first do this, you'll probably have 13 or more values. Now, look through the list of values and see if any of them are similar or something you can combine, so you get down to about seven values. These are your core values.

Now that you have your core values, you can write a sentence or two to determine how these values show up in your life. Here are a few examples from my family's core values list.

- **Respect:** We show each other respect. We use kind words when talking to each other and maintain respect, even when we argue.
- **Playful:** We are a playful family. We find the fun in any situation and enjoy keeping our youthful spirit.
- **Integrity:** We say what we mean, and we mean what we say. We hold ourselves to a high standard, to be honest, because our word means something.

Now, do we always live up to our values? The honest answer is no. But they are still a guiding principle for how we choose to act. And they are always a reminder of what we want our family to stand for.

It's okay to have different values in different areas of your life. My business has core values that are different from my family's or my personal values. You can have similar, overlapping, or even different values for all the areas of your life you choose to do this exercise for.

Beliefs and values are at the same level as they both influence each other. Your beliefs can influence your values and vice versa. If you have a belief that doesn't serve you, see if there's an underlying value that either isn't there or needs to be adjusted.

Identity

These are your "I am" statements. They are who you are. If you are working on an issue and you've worked through every other layer, it may be time to look at your "I am" statements. What do you tell yourself, your friends, and your coworkers that start with "I am"?

Remember the story of my friend who didn't like it when I said, "I am stupid"? I had to work hard to remove that phrase from my vocabulary. I first had to decide what I wanted instead. If I didn't want to be stupid, what *did* I want to be? I wanted to be smart. Next, I had to make it an "I am" statement. "I am smart".

You must first decide what you want instead of what is currently in place. You can work with your inner child to determine this, as they are very good at wanting the best for you. Make your statements as short as possible. I am smart. I am someone who works out. I am healthy. I am someone who reads every day. I am someone who dresses well. I am loved. I am someone who loves. The possibilities are endless. Be creative and determine who you want to be.

Once you have your new identity statement, you can follow the process outlined below to install it into your subconscious.

1. State your phrase to yourself every morning (and randomly throughout the day as needed).
2. Notice when you say your old phrase and correct it immediately after you notice it.
3. Be consistent with this. It may take time, but consistency is what will change it for you.

You may not know when the change will happen, but one day, you'll wake up and just notice that you haven't said your old phrase in a long time. You just *are* your new identity.

Spirit

These are the rules, standards, and guidelines from a higher power. You may call it God, Yahweh, Allah, the heavens, source, spirit, your deity, the universe, manifestation, quantum physics, etc. You can call it what you want, but these are the guiding principles given to us we live our lives by. You have less influence on this than you do on other neurological levels, and it is the very last layer to look at if your change has not stuck.

EMBRACING IMPERFECTION

It is an uncomfortable truth that nothing is perfect. That means we need to get comfortable with imperfection. No matter how many times you have done something, how many times you've checked something, or how long you've been with someone, it's not perfect. There is almost always room for improvement, ways to get better, or even mistakes.

I started writing my first book in 2014. This book is still in draft form and barely has over four chapters finished because it had to be perfect. Since then, I've changed my focus, developed more experience and tools, and even received some amazing advice from people I know, love, and trust. So, that "perfect" book will probably always remain a could-have-been.

I'm sure some people have read this book and found some errors. It's okay. Even though a lot of time and attention has gone into fixing the big, glaring ones, I still find something I want to improve. This is great news because it gives me the chance to update the content, provide better information over time, and still give readers the tools they need to change their lives.

Perfectionism, or the pursuit of perfection, opens the door for harsh self-judgment. This might look like not turning a project in on time because it isn't quite perfect or canceling plans because you don't look good enough to go out. When you push yourself toward perfection, you put your body into "danger" mode regularly.

Why? If we're constantly chasing something that doesn't exist or that isn't achievable, there is no end in sight. Imagine going for a run, but you don't know how long or how far you're going. In fact, there is no end to your run. Once you start, you just keep running, just like Forrest Gump did in the 1994 film. What do you think happens to the body if it's always in go mode? If it's always stressing over fixing something until it's perfect?

There are 1.9 billion results on Google for the phrase "What does stress do to the body?" That number increases by a whopping 836 million results when we search about stress and the mind. But let's take this one step further.

If you've ever felt like you're not good enough, you may know exactly what impact perfectionism had on your inner child. If you've ever felt like you could do something better or were expected to never make a mistake, you know the impact. And often, that idea stays with us into our adulthood, where we continue to expect a high standard.

When you demand too much of yourself, you send a message to your inner child that you accept nothing less than the best. Your inner child receives this harmful message, and they may react in a way that's not helpful or useful in the situation you're in.

Take a moment and let yourself and your inner child know it's okay to mess up. It's okay to make mistakes. There are very few mistakes, errors, or imperfections that cannot be adjusted or fixed along the way. When your inner child feels safe and like you're in control and not needlessly stressing, they are less likely to take the wheel and cause a scene.

HOW TO EMBRACE IMPERFECTIONS

If you've ever spent some time with someone who expects perfection, you may know how exhausting that relationship can be. Not to mention how tightly wound they are at times. It most likely takes very little to get them to fly off the handle. If this is you, it's ok. I'm not saying you need to accept shoddy work, low standards, or put yourself in danger from taking risks. There is a difference between a mistake and a repeated behavior.

Our flaws and imperfections make us human. They are there regardless of how high a standard we place on ourselves and others. The ability to embrace those flaws is a sign of a truly healed person.

Tips for Embracing Imperfection

- **Use your flaws to relate to others.** After all, we are not alone in this! Realize that everyone struggles and everyone makes mistakes. Let this be a bridge that connects you to others. This can sound like relating to someone else who made a mistake. "When I was your age, I made a similar mistake..." or "I've been where you are, here's how I handled it..."
- **Set realistic standards for yourself.** Instead of saying something like, "I will have a 60-minute workout

at the gym every day," give yourself some wiggle room and start off with something you're likely to achieve. When you first start out, maybe say something like, "I will work out for 20 minutes a day at home or at the gym." This gives you something you can achieve and maintain. And if you make a mistake, it's not because you went too big right out the gate.
- **Don't compare yourself to others.** I can't stress this enough. You have no idea what is going on in someone's life or mind. That is why playing the comparison game will always make you feel awful. Besides, you may compare your first chapter to someone else's middle or last chapter. We don't always see everyone else's struggle to get where they are.
- **Reframe your negative thoughts:** Did you catch yourself saying something that wasn't nice? Time to reframe it! Instead of "I really messed up in that meeting earlier," try something like, "I had a bit of a setback in that meeting earlier. But I am learning from it and growing." Don't let the negative thoughts just go! Reframe it into something more compassionate and positive.

SIGNS YOU ARE HEALING YOUR INNER CHILD

The great thing about healing your inner child is when you experience the benefits of your hard work. While the process itself is rewarding, we all want to see results, right? Since your journey is unique, the timing of your results may vary. But there are several ways your life will change for the better after reintegrating with your inner child. Whenever you doubt your progress, look back and remember your starting point. Celebrate even the tiny wins.

Here are a few examples of moments you will notice on your journey.

- You connect more with your emotional and physical sensations.
- You improve in identifying and communicating your emotions.
- You make time for play.
- You find you're more creative and joyful.
- You have less drastic mood changes.
- You enjoy spending time with yourself and others more than you did before.
- You enjoy life and become the person you want to be.

These incredible benefits come from connecting with your inner child, acknowledging their pain, and seeking a path forward. When you begin to reparent your inner child and change your thought patterns, you find that almost anything in life is possible. So, dream big!

EXERCISE: CIRCLE OF EXCELLENCE (RING OF POWER)!

This is one of my absolute favorite exercises, and I saved it until the end because so much of what we learn in this book is enhanced by going through this process. It will give you the ability to try on a new you, amplify and have ready access to a positive emotional resource, or step into the person you want to be.

You need little space for this one, but you need a clean, open area in front of you. Before you begin the exercise, decide on the emotion (or list of emotions) you want instantly accessible. Some common emotions and resources I've used this exercise for are happiness, peace, creativity, focus, and relaxation. I also use this exercise to define the person I want to be. Examples are the ability to effortlessly make sales calls, the power and excitement to speak on stage, and the person who is strong enough to have a hard and needed conversation. And so many more!

1. Imagine an invisible circle on the floor, 3 feet wide and 2 feet out in front of you.
2. Without moving, go inside your mind and recall a time when you had what you wanted—where you were wonderful. Everything was going smoothly. You were bright, witty, capable, and had success. *Note: If you do not have a personal history of this resource, you may simply pretend that you have the history and proceed. Or you may use any other person's history. You can use a movie hero, a living or dead legend, or anyone you admire. The amazing thing about your brain is that it can't tell the difference between real and imagined personal history or the history of others. Go ahead. No one will know.*
3. Develop a full, dissociated visual and kinesthetic representation of this state. See yourself in the circle, being wonderful. Hear yourself responding the way you desire. Feel yourself gushing with pride.
4. Step into the circle and take a visual picture of yourself. Allow yourself to feel, see, and hear everything you created in the circle. *Note: Your whole body should change as you step into the visual picture you created. If you are working with the emotion of happiness, you should have the overwhelming urge to smile. If you are working with confidence, you should have the overwhelming urge to stand tall. Your body should naturally take on the feelings and emotions of the picture you created. Let yourself experience this moment.*

5. Take a step back out of the circle. Did it feel the way you wanted it to feel? Is there more you need to add to it? More detail? More intensity? More resources? Add the additional detail into the visual representation of you inside the circle. Step back in and test it out again.
6. Repeat steps 3-5 as needed until you've got it exactly where you feel a strong connection to the resource.
7. While standing in the middle of the circle and feeling the strong connection to the resource, anchor this feeling to somewhere you can have easy access whenever you desire. My favorite way to anchor this experience is with my non-dominant hand. I use my middle fingertip, pointer-finger fingertip, and the tip of my thumb. I hold all of those together as my anchor.
8. Now, whenever you need to access that emotion, activate your anchor by placing your fingertips together using the same amount of pressure as when you set the anchor.

This exercise does not create competence. It can, however, provide you with a dose of competence. The more you trigger this resource, the more you act as if you already have this resource, and the more it will be available for you over time.

CONCLUSION

The inner child within all of us is calling out for recognition and acknowledgment and desperately wants to see you become the best version of yourself. By reading this book and going through the process, you have answered that call! This is not a small thing, and I want you to be proud of the work that you have done so far. There are many significant benefits to reparenting and reconnecting with your inner child, and I've listed several of them throughout the book.

I've done my best to lay everything out in an easy-to-read and easy-to-follow manner. Don't get discouraged if you need to go back and reread an exercise, a paragraph, or a chapter. Do the work on yourself and reap the benefits of a healed inner child who works with you instead of doing everything they can to get your attention.

Healing is a journey. It takes time to clean up years of pushing your emotions aside. It takes time to discover who you want to be. It takes time to reconnect with your inner child and create a healthy working relationship with it. It's time well spent.

You don't have to live your life at the mercy of your emotions or with an 8-year-old in the driver's seat. Using the tips and tricks you have learned, you can begin healing those childhood wounds and becoming the best version of yourself.

The events of your childhood cannot be changed or undone. The past is the past. However, you now know the steps to address the residual pain, stuck emotions, and unresourceful responses your past left for you. That is a tremendous step in the right direction. Don't lose sight of where you want to be. Continue to connect with all the pieces of your past. Continue to work with yourself at every age along the way. You and all your parts have gotten you this far. Thank them, love them, accept them, and work with them to create a future designed by you.

This is *your* time. May your journey be as unique and as rewarding as it has been for me and countless other people. You are a beautiful soul, and you deserve to become who you are meant to be.

LOOKING FOR ADDITIONAL RESOURCES?

If you're struggling to develop a healthy relationship with your inner child or you want an experienced guide to help you through the process, I'd be delighted to help.

I have a coaching program that helps you take the concepts in this book and apply them directly to your life. This program is hands-on and works with the root of what's stopping you from getting what you want out of life. It's perfect for anyone who reacts to situations instead of controlling their response in a helpful, purposeful way. It works for everyone, from stay-at-home moms to CEOs and entrepreneurs and everyone in between.

This isn't therapy, and it isn't a 'bash your parents' program. It's a way to reconnect with your inner child and reparent them the way you need to live the life you've always wanted. If that sounds like you and you're ready to take the next step in becoming the person you want to be, visit the Inner Child Coaching Program, at www.vitalskillspress.com/innerchild-resources and let's chat. I would love to meet you and see how we can help you break the barriers that hold you back from whatever you want in life.

ACKNOWLEDGMENTS

This book wouldn't have happened without the help of some amazing people in my life. Thank you to everyone along the way who helped me grow and pushed me out of my comfort zone. Thank you to everyone who read and reviewed my manuscript repeatedly until you could almost recite it by heart. Thank you to Susan Stageman for not only introducing me to NLP but also helping me through some very tough and difficult times as a coach and a friend. A special thank you to my family for putting up with some of the long nights in my office tapping away on my computer. Daniel, Aiden, Renee, Mackenzie, and Marilyn, I'm excited to be fully present during family time again. Thank you to my parents for their unwavering support of all the crazy things I've wanted to do in life. I wouldn't be the woman I am today without both of you. Finally, this wouldn't be a true book about the inner child if I didn't acknowledge my inner child, who is still alive and well inside. She would like to thank the one person who read this entire book waiting to see if they would be mentioned, and as promised, you are here at the end of the book. You know who you are!

NOTES:

1. Aletheia. "25 Signs You Have a Wounded Inner Child(+ How to Heal)." LonerWolf, April 6, 2019. https://lonerwolf.com/feeling-safe-inner-child/.
2. alex.haslam.writing@gmail.com. "How to Create Your Own Safe Space at Home." Thrive Global, August 14, 2018. https://community.thriveglobal.com/how-to-create-your-own-safe-space-at-home/.
3. BalboaPress. "#LoveYourself," n.d. http://www.balboapress.com/en/bookstore/bookdetails/720450-loveyourself.
4. "*Barbie* (Film)." In *Wikipedia*, n.d. https://en.wikipedia.org/w/index.php?title=Barbie_(film)&oldid=1202858866.
5. CNET. "Top 3 Reasons to Show Yourself Compassion This Year, and How to Start," n.d. https://www.cnet.com/health/mental/top-3-reasons-to-show-your self-compassion-this-year-and-how-to-start/.
6. "Coaching Tool Kit: Neurological Levels." Grow the Coach, 2020. https://growthecoach.com/wp-content/uploads/2020/04/Neurological-levels.pdf .
7. Cummings, E. E. *E. E. Cummings: A Miscellany Revised*. First Edition. October House, 1965.
8. Curtis, T. (2023, January 10). 6 ways to set financial boundaries. NerdWallet. https://www.nerdwallet.com/article/finance/setting-boundaries
9. Darcy, Andrea M. "What Is the 'Inner Child'?" Harley Therapy™ Blog, March 23, 2017. https://www.harleytherapy.co.uk/counselling/what-is-the-inner-child.htm.
10. Doyle, Glennon, and Glennon Doyle Melton. *Untamed*. Later Printing edition. New York: The Dial Press, 2020.
11. Dr. Su Yin Yap. "Headstuff." *The Importance of Self-Compassion* (blog), April 3, 2018. https://headstuff.org/topical/science/psychology/mind-your-mind-the-importance-of-self-compassion/.
12. Gaba, S. (2020, December 16). Carrying a wounded inner child into your relationships?. Psychology Today. https://www.psychologytoday.com/us/blog/addiction-and-recovery/202012/carrying-wounded-inner-child-your-relationships
13. "How To Heal Your Inner Child In Seven Steps | Solara Mental Health," November 7, 2019. https://solaramentalhealth.com/heal-your-inner-child/.
14. "Is Nonverbal Communication a Numbers Game? | Psychology Today," n.d. https://www.psychologytoday.com/us/blog/beyond-words/201109/is-nonverbal-communication-a-numbers-game.
15. Karefilakis, Maria. "Kare Psychology—The Conscious and Subconscious

Mind." *Kare Psychology* (blog), February 22, 2019. https://karepsychology.com.au/the-conscious-and-subconscious-mind/.
16. Kids Help Phone. "10 Ways to Practice Self-Acceptance," n.d. https://kidshelpphone.ca/get-info/10-ways-practice-self-acceptance/
17. Kim. (2018, March 26). NLP anchoring. NLP Mentor. https://nlp-mentor.com/nlp-anchoring/
18. Lion's Roar. "Thich Nhat Hanh on Healing the Child Within," n.d. https://www.lionsroar.com/healing-the-child-within/.
19. Lively, K. J. (2013, November 2). Why women have a hard time saying no. Psychology Today. https://www.psychologytoday.com/us/blog/smart-relationships/201311/why-women-have-hard-time-saying-no
20. "Love Publishing Technology Blog Posts with HackerNoon | HackerNoon," n.d. https://hackernoon.com/p/publish.
21. MA, Hokuma Karimova. "The Emotion Wheel: What It Is and How to Use It." PositivePsychology.com, December 24, 2017. https://positivepsychology.com/emotion-wheel/.
22. Martin, Dr Sharon. "What Are Boundaries and Why Do I Need Them?" *Live Well with Sharon Martin* (blog), April 24, 2018. https://www.livewellwithsharonmartin.com/what-are-boundaries/.
23. Mas, Sira. "4 Examples of Boundary Violations." *The Truly Charming* (blog), August 7, 2022. https://thetrulycharming.com/examples-of-boundary-violations/.
24. Miller, Michael. "Getting Unstuck: The Power of Naming Emotions." Six Seconds, January 8, 2021. https://www.6seconds.org/2021/01/08/getting-unstuck-power-naming-emotions/.
25. "[PDF] Chapter 3. Inner Child Work and Codependency—Free Download PDF," n.d. https://silo.tips/download/chapter-3-inner-child-work-and-codependency.
26. PhD, Rivka Edery. "Non-Dominant Handwriting as a Way to Access Parts— PARTS & SELF," April 13, 2023. https://partsandself.org/non-dominant-handwriting-as-a-way-to-access-parts/, https://partsandself.org/non-dominant-handwriting-as-a-way-to-access-parts/.
27. Psych Central. "7 Types of Boundaries You May Need," April 23, 2020. https://psychcentral.com/blog/imperfect/2020/04/7-types-of-boundaries-you-may-need.
28. Psych Central. "17 Boundaries Quotes," June 5, 2016. https://psychcentral.com/health/quotes-healthy-boundaries.
29. Purkayastha, Rajashree. "9 Inner Child Quotes That Will Make You Come Alive." *Medium* (blog), November 18, 2022. https://medium.com/@mail2rajashree/9-inner-child-quotes-that-will-make-you-come-alive-3f7fa03cc2b4.
30. "Reparenting to Heal the Wounded Inner Child | CPTSDfoundation.Org,"

n.d. https://cptsdfoundation.org/2020/07/27/reparenting-to-heal-the-wounded-inner-child/.
31. Roggero, V. (2022, August 3). 7 Types Of Inner Child: Which Archetype Are You? Vivienroggero.com; Viviene Roggero. https://vivienroggero.com/blog/types-of-inner-child
32. Schmidt, Katharina. "Council Post: Why Naming Your Emotions Can Increase Happiness And Performance." Forbes, n.d. https://www.forbes.com/sites/forbescoachescouncil/2021/08/31/why-naming-your-emotions-can-increase-happiness-and-performance/.
33. Seymour, Laurie. "Dream Boldly: 10 Questions to Rouse Your Inner Child Wisdom." The Baca Institute, December 5, 2014. https://thebacainstitute.com/dream-boldly-rouse-inner-child-wisdom/.
34. Silk + Sonder. "6 Powerful Steps for How to Heal Your Inner Child," April 10, 2023. https://www.silkandsonder.com/blogs/news/6-powerful-steps-for-how-to-heal-your-inner-child.
35. Staff, iNLP Center. "NLP Techiques: Basic Anchoring in 5 Simple Steps." iNLP Center, June 6, 2018. https://inlpcenter.org/nlp-anchoring/.
36. Stevelos, J. (2021, August 10). Sexual abuse and obesity - what's The link? Obesity Action Coalition. https://www.obesityaction.org/resources/sexual-abuse-and-obesity-whats-the-link/
37. "That Giant Tarantula Is Terrifying, but I'll Touch It," n.d. https://www.uclahealth.org/news/that-giant-tarantula-is-terrifying-but-ill-touch-it.
38. TIME. "What to Know About Inner Child Work," April 6, 2023. https://time.com/6268636/inner-child-work-healing/.
39. tonyrobbins.com. "How to Surround Yourself with Good People," n.d. https://www.tonyrobbins.com/stories/business-mastery/surround-yourself-with-quality-people/.
40. UWA. "Science of Emotion: The Basics of Emotional Psychology | UWA." UWA Online, June 27, 2019. https://online.uwa.edu/news/emotional-psychology/.
41. Verywell Mind. "The Important Role of Emotions," n.d. https://www.verywellmind.com/the-purpose-of-emotions-2795181.
42. Weis, F. (2020, March 20). Confidence is the result of experience. Thrive Global. https://community.thriveglobal.com/confidence-is-the-result-of-experience-2
43. wikiHow. "3 Ways to Create a Safe Place in Your Mind," n.d. https://www.wikihow.com/Create-a-Safe-Place-in-Your-Mind.

www.ingramcontent.com/pod-product-compliance
Lightning Source LLC
Chambersburg PA
CBHW030335010526
44119CB00028B/403/J